S0-ADF-125

PRESIDENTIAL INAUGURATIONS

Inauguration of President Polk. Here, in the words of John Quincy Adams, "Mr. Polk delivered his inaugural address . . . to a large assemblage of umbrellas." From the *Illustrated London News*—see items 1 and 602.

Presidential Inaugurations

A Selected List of References

THIRD EDITION, REVISED AND ENLARGED

Compiled by RUTH S. FREITAG

Bibliography and Reference Correspondence Section
General Reference and Bibliography Division
REFERENCE DEPARTMENT

THE LIBRARY OF CONGRESS • WASHINGTON

1969

L.C. Card 76-602825

For sale by the Superintendent of Documents
U.S. Government Printing Office
Washington, D.C. 20402 - Price $2

PREFACE

Scope. The present list is a complete revision and updating of the 1960 edition of *Presidential Inaugurations* and its 1964 supplement, both compiled by the General Reference and Bibliography Division. Following the practice begun in 1949, this third edition has been prepared to serve as a guide to information on inaugural ceremonies and festivities from 1789 to the present.

Although the emphasis is on books, parts of books, and periodical articles, many items from newspapers are also cited. Since the fixed date of the ceremonies makes newspaper coverage relatively simple to trace, comprehensive inclusion of this material was not attempted. Nor are references included to the Library's holdings of motion pictures and sound recordings relating to inaugurations.

While an effort was made to call attention to the presence of pictures in the cited publications, it was not possible to include references to the large quantity of illustrative materials in the Presidential file of the Library's Prints and Photographs Division. Some of these are listed in the second edition of *Pictorial Americana,* compiled by Milton Kaplan and edited by Charles G. LaHood, Jr. (Washington, Library of Congress, 1955. 68 p.).

Arrangement. As the table of contents indicates, the list comprises a general section, six sections on specific topics, and a section on the inaugurations of individual Presidents. Arrangement in each section and subsection is alphabetical, with the exception of "Invitations, Programs, and Other Memorabilia," the arrangement of which is primarily chronological. An index to authors and subjects completes the work.

Location of items is indicated either by a Library of Congress call number or location symbol, or, for material in another library, by the National Union Catalog symbol for that library.

Many references will be found to items in the District of Columbia Public Library. These materials are all in the Washingtoniana Collection at the central library; they are at present organized into seven scrapbooks and five file boxes containing folders for each President, for the subject as a whole, and for special aspects such as Bibles, inaugural balls, and the weather. Specific locations have been given for items in this collection that are described here.

A supplement covering material published for the 1969 inauguration has been added. Items in this supplement are not indexed.

KEY TO SYMBOLS

Library of Congress Symbols

LL	Law Library
Micro	Microfilm Reading Room
Mss	Manuscript Division
Newsp	Newspaper Reading Room
P&P	Prints and Photographs Division
Rare Bk. Coll.	Rare Book Collection

National Union Catalog Symbols

DWP	District of Columbia Public Library
ICN	Newberry Library, Chicago
MiU-C	William L. Clements Library, University of Michigan, Ann Arbor
RPB	Brown University, Providence, R.I.

CONTENTS

PRESIDENTIAL INAUGURATIONS

GENERAL

1

Adams, John Quincy, *Pres. U.S.* Memoirs, comprising portions of his diary from 1795 to 1848. Edited by Charles Francis Adams. Philadelphia, J. B. Lippincott, 1874-77. 12 v. illus. E377.A19

The following inaugurations are described: Jefferson's second, v. 1, p. 373; Madison's first, v. 1, p. 544; Monroe's second, v. 5, p. 317-318; J. Q. Adams, v. 6, p. 518-519; W. H. Harrison, v. 10, p. 439-440; Tyler, v. 10, p. 458; Polk, v. 12, p. 178-179.

2

Aikman, Lonnelle. We, the people; the story of the United States Capitol, its past and its promise. [Washington] United States Capitol Historical Society, 1963. 143 p. illus. (part col.) F204.C2A45

Includes scattered information and pictures on a few inaugurations; *see* index.

3

Album of American history [by] James Truslow Adams, editor in chief [and others] New York, Scribner, 1944-61. 6 v. illus., maps, ports. E178.5.A48

"The intent of the present work is to tell the history of America through pictures made at the time the history was being made."

Contents. v. 1. Colonial period. v. 2. 1783-1853. v. 3. 1853-1893. v. 4. End of an era. v. 5. 1917-1953; editor: J. G. E. Hopkins. Index (rev. ed., 1961).

Pictures of inaugurations are given in v. 2-5 as listed in the index.

4

Anderson, Isabel W. (Perkins). Presidents and pies; life in Washington, 1897-1919. Boston, Houghton Mifflin Co., 1920. 290 p. illus. F199.A56

Inauguration of Taft: p. 98-103.

Wilson's second inauguration: p. 180-184.

5

Andrews, Dorothea. President in his own right: Harry, like T. R., no accident this time. Washington post, Jan. 20, 1949: 2C, 14C. illus.
Newsp

Includes a number of details about other inaugurations.

6

The artist as a recorder of historical events. Art education, v. 18, Jan. 1965: 9-11. N81.A86, v. 18

Reproduces some engravings showing scenes of past Presidential inaugurations, from the pages of mid-19th-century periodicals. Another illustration on cover.

7

Baer, Frank L. Inaugurals are hard on Presidents. Evening star (Washington), Jan. 21, 1953: A-18. illus. Newsp

8

Banister, Margaret. This democratic world. Washingtonian, Mar. 1929: 20-22, 50. illus. F191.W39, 1929

Reviews history of earlier inaugurals.

9

Banister, Margaret. Inaugurations—past and present. Democratic bulletin, v. 8, Mar. 1933: 30-33, 46-47, 50. illus. JK2311.D35, v. 8

10

Barbee, David R. Chief Justice Marshall swore in 9 Presidents. *In* The Washington post. Inaugural edition, Saturday, March 4, 1933. Washington, 1933. p. 18. E806.W28

11

Barbee, David R. Inaugurals ban religious rites; no invocation, no benediction, except in case of Washington's. *In* The Washington post. Inaugural edition, Saturday, March 4, 1933. Washington, 1933. p. 15.
E806.W28

12
Barbee, David R. Roosevelt to be seventh inaugurated on Saturday. *In* The Washington post. Inaugural edition, Saturday, March 4, 1933. Washington, 1933. p. 11. E806.W28

Table shows which Presidents were inaugurated on each day of the week.

13
Baughman, Urbanus E. Secret Service Chief, by U. E. Baughman, with Leonard Wallace Robinson. New York, Harper [1962] 266 p. illus. HV8138.B3

Kennedy's inauguration: p. 1-4.
"Inaugural Dangers": p. 41-53.

14
Behind the inaugural mike. Newsweek, v. 33, Jan. 31, 1949: 49. port. AP2.N6772, v. 33

Experiences of Bob Trout in broadcasting the last five inaugurations.

15
Berliner, Milton. As it was in the other days. Washington daily news, Jan. 20, 1949: 55, 57. illus. Newsp

16
Binkley, Wilfred E. Inauguration of the President. *In* Adams, James Truslow, *ed.* Dictionary of American history. 2d ed., rev. v. 3. New York, C. Scribner's Sons [1942] p. 81-82. E174.A43 1942

17
Bishop, Joseph B. Inauguration scenes and incidents. Century magazine, v. 53, Mar. 1897: 733-740. illus. AP2.C4, v. 53

18
Bishop, Joseph B. Our political drama, conventions, campaigns, candidates; with numerous illustrations and reproductions from caricatures. New York, Scott Thaw Co., 1904. 236 p. JK2261.B59

Three articles entitled "Humor and Pathos of National Conventions," "Scenes and Incidents of Presidential Inaugurations," and "Early Political Caricature in America," published originally in the *Century Magazine*, form the basis of the present volume.

19

Bishop, Joseph B. Presidential nominations and elections; a history of American conventions, national campaigns, inaugurations and campaign caricature, with numerous illustrations. New York, C. Scribner's Sons, 1916. 237 p. plates. JK2261.B6

"A portion of the material in this volume appeared in a book published by me in 1904, entitled *'Our Political Drama'* ... To it has been added sufficient new matter to present a complete review ... down to the present time."–Preface.

20

Brant, Theron L. The fourth of March; the drama of our Presidential inaugurations. Everybody's magazine, v. 12, Mar. 1905: 371-376.
AP2.E9, v. 12

21

Brown, George R. Inaugural ceremony has marked high spot through American history. Washington herald, Mar. 4, 1933: 2-B. illus.
Newsp

22

Brown, George R. 1789-1929: the story of our Presidents as told by inauguration days for 140 years. *In* The Washington post. Inaugural edition, Monday, March 4, 1929. Washington, 1929. p. 1-5, 8-10, 13-22, 25-35, 41-46. illus. E801.W31

23

Brown, George R. Washington, a not too serious history. Baltimore, Norman Pub. Co., 1930. 481 p. illus. F194.B872

Inaugurations: Jefferson's first, p. 52-56; Madison's first, p. 230-232; Monroe's first, p. 125-128; J. Q. Adams, p. 246-249; Jackson's first, p. 258-262; Van Buren, p. 283-286; W. H. Harrison, p. 289; Tyler, p. 290.

Inaugural ball of 1809: p. 119-121.

An illustration showing Pennsylvania Avenue at Sixth Street during the inauguration of President Pierce appears opposite p. 198.

24

Bryan, Wilhelmus B. A history of the National Capital from its foundation through the period of the adoption of the organic act. New York, Macmillan Co., 1914-16. 2 v. illus., maps, plans. F194.B9

Contents. 1. 1790-1814. 2. 1815-1878.
See index under Inaugurations.

25
Burr, Kate. Presidential inaugurations, past and present. National monthly, v. 4, Mar. 1913: 243, 255-256. AP2.N348, v. 4

26
Catton, Bruce. "... So help me God." This week, Jan. 20, 1957: 2. illus. Newsp

Available on microfilm of *Sunday Star* (Washington).

27
Cavalcade of inaugurations. New York times magazine, Jan. 16, 1949: 8-9. illus. AP2.N6575, 1949

Scenes from the inaugurations of 1789, 1801, 1829, 1865, 1885, 1905, 1913, and 1933.

28
Chance, William W. Policing the inauguration crowds. Sunday star (Washington), Mar. 5, 1933, pt. 7: 37. illus. Newsp

29
Chapin, Elizabeth (Moore). American court gossip; or, Life at the National Capitol [!] Marshalltown, Ia., Chapin & Hartwell Bros., 1887. 269 p. F199.C46

Garfield's inauguration: p. 46-48.
Cleveland's first inauguration: p. 194-199.

30
Cline, John H. Bringing the crowds to Washington. Sunday star (Washington), Mar. 5, 1933, pt. 7: 26, 41. illus. Newsp

How the Presidents and others made their way to the Capital for the inauguration.

31
Colman, Edna M. (Hercher). Inaugurals of a century. Washington post, Feb. 28, 1909, magazine section: 10. illus. Newsp

32

Colman, Edna M. (Hercher). Seventy-five years of White House gossip. Garden City, N.Y., Doubleday, Page, 1925. 334 p. plates, ports. E176.1.C75

A chapter is devoted to each Presidential administration from Washington through Lincoln. A description of the inauguration ceremonies and festivities is given at or near the beginning of every chapter.

33

Colman, Edna M. (Hercher). White House gossip, from Andrew Johnson to Calvin Coolidge. Garden City, N.Y., Doubleday, Page, 1927. 431 p. plates, ports. E176.1.C76

Continues the pattern of her *Seventy-five Years of White House Gossip,* ending with the first administration of Coolidge.

34

Commager, Henry S. "To preserve, protect, and defend." Senior scholastic, v. 53, Jan. 19, 1949: 11. illus. AP2.S477, v. 53

35

Custom. New Yorker, v. 24, Jan. 22, 1949: 17-19. AP2.N6763, v. 24

Includes some information about floats.

36

Daniel, Frederick S. Inaugurations and coronations. Cosmopolitan, v. 14, Apr. 1893: 715-723. illus. AP2.C8, v 14

37

De Blois, Frank. Inauguration day; a great American tradition comes to life next Thursday. Parade, Jan. 16, 1949: 16-17. illus. AP2.P263, 1949

38

Dixon, Mason J. Our inaugural precedents. National republic, v. 32, Jan. 1945: 1-3, 31. illus. E171.N32, v. 32

39

Doyle, Burton T., *and* Homer H. Swaney. Lives of James A. Garfield and Chester A. Arthur. With a brief sketch of the assassin. Washington, R. H. Darby, 1881. 224 p. plates, ports. E687.D75

Garfield's inauguration: p. 47-55.

Arthur's inauguration: p. 194-195.

"Appendix A. Inaugurations from Washington to Garfield": p. 203-217.

40

Drury, Martin L. Presidential inaugurations. American homes and gardens, v. 10, Mar. 1913: xxiv-xxvii. NA7100.A55, v. 10

41

Durant, John, *and* Alice K. (Rand) Durant. Pictorial history of American Presidents. 4th rev. ed. New York, A. S. Barnes [1965] 356 p. illus. E176.1.D9 1965

Includes information on inaugurations of some Presidents. *See* index.

42

Eberlein, Harold D., *and* Cortlandt V. Hubbard. Diary of Independence Hall. Philadelphia, J. B. Lippincott Co. [1948] 378 p. illus., map. F158.8.I3E3

Washington's second inauguration: p. 322-323.

Inauguration of John Adams: p. 336-337.

43

Eberlein, Harold D., *and* Cortlandt V. Hubbard. Historic houses of George-Town & Washington City. Richmond, Dietz Press [1958] 480 p. illus., map. F195.E2

Chapter on the White House gives information on the following inaugurations: Monroe's second, p. 214; J. Q. Adams, p. 217; Jackson's first, p. 226-228; Van Buren, p. 232.

44

Eiselen, Malcolm R. "Preserve, protect, and defend–" North American review, v. 242, winter 1936/37: 334-349. AP2.N7, v. 242

45

Ellis, John B. The sights and secrets of the National Capital: a work descriptive of Washington City in all its various phases. New York, United States Pub. Co., 1869. xix, 512 p. illus. F198.E47

Another edition published in Chicago the same year.

Inaugurations: p. 219-224.

46

Emerson, Edwin. Inaugurations of the past. Leslie's weekly, v. 84, Mar. 11, 1897: 155. AP2.L52, v. 84

47

Epic of America written in its inaugurals. New York times magazine, Jan. 17, 1937: 14-15. illus. AP2.N6575, 1937

48

Evans, Jessie F. History records many changes in inauguration procedure. Sunday star (Washington), Jan. 19, 1941, pt. 1: 15. port. Newsp

49

Famous firsts. Evening star (Washington), Jan. 21, 1957, inaugural souvenir section: 12. illus. Newsp

50

Famous inaugurals of other days; spectacular parades, flowery speeches, great balls, marked the occasion. World review, v. 8, Mar. 4, 1929: 69. illus. AP2.W7487, v. 8

51

Fenton, Edward. Radio, telegraph carry ceremony to Nation's far corners; public once waited weeks to hear story. Washington post, Jan. 20, 1937: B-9. Newsp

52

Fincher, Ernest B. The President of the United States. New York, Abelard-Schuman [1955] 192 p. illus. JK516.F48

Inaugurations: p. [54]-62.

53

Fitch, George. Some timid suggestions for the preservation of the inaugural ceremonies. Collier's, v. 50, Mar. 8, 1913: 15, 26, 28. illus. AP2.C65, v. 50

About parades.

54

Fleming, Thomas. Around the Capital with Uncle Hank, recorded together with many pictures. New York, Nutshell Pub. Co., 1902. 346 p. illus. F199.F59

"Inauguration Day": p. 183-190. Describes the events of a typical inauguration day.

55

Fleming, Thomas. The Capital; a book about the City of Washington and the public men thereof. [New York] Capital Cartoon Syndicate, 1913. 398 p. illus. F199.F6

"Inauguration Day": p. 189-201. Revision of preceding entry.

56

Foley, James P. She remembers 18 Presidents. American weekly, Jan. 20, 1957: 2. illus. AP2.A464, 1957

About Mrs. Nettie Moulden, who attended every inaugural from 1865 to 1953.

57

Folliard, Edward T. On Sunday inaugurals: 2 other Presidents sworn in privately. Washington post, Jan. 19, 1957: B-1. Newsp

58

Ford, Elizabeth. Inaugural tales: every quadrennial has its distinctive incident which has found place in annals of successive holders of leadership. Evening star (Washington), Jan. 16, 1937: B-1. Newsp

59

Former inaugurations; from Washington to Cleveland, how the Presidents have been installed in office. Evening star (Washington), Mar. 3, 1885: 2. Newsp

60

Fraser, Hugh R. Democracy in the making; the Jackson-Tyler era. Indianapolis, Bobbs-Merrill Co. [c1938] 334 p. illus. E338.F73

Van Buren's inauguration: p. 77.
Harrison's inauguration: p. 138.
Tyler's inauguration: p. 151-153, 157-159.

61

Freed, Clyde H. Some notes on early inaugurations and the part our railroad played in them. Baltimore and Ohio employes magazine, v. 4, Feb. 1917: 23-25. TF1.B3, v. 4

325-882 O-69—2

62

From Lincoln to Harrison–1861-1889; a review of the Republican Presidential inaugurations. Frank Leslie's illustrated newspaper, v. 68, Mar. 9, 1889: 70, 75, 78. illus. AP2.L52, v. 68

63

From the beginning: first inauguration and that of Roosevelt. Growth of function; selection of March 4 purely without design. Always has been a ball–raid during Grant's first festivities. Evening star (Washington), Mar. 4, 1905, pt. 2: 1. Newsp

64

Furman, Bess. White House profile; a social history of the White House, its occupants and its festivities. Indianapolis, Bobbs-Merrill [c1951] 368 p. illus. F204.W5F8

Contains scattered brief information on the inaugurations of various Presidents, some of which is indexed under their names.

65

Gage, Earle W. Inauguration of the President. National republic, v. 44, Jan. 1957: 5-6. illus. E171.N32, v. 44

66

George, Alexander R. Inaugural pageant: Washington to Hoover. Evening star (Washington), Jan. 31, 1929: 49; Feb. 1: 40; Feb. 2: 18; Feb. 4: 27; Feb. 5: 36; Feb. 6: 32; Feb; 7: 43; Feb. 8: 38; Feb. 9: 22; Feb. 11: 28; Feb. 12: 28; Feb. 13: 30; Feb. 14: 54; Feb. 15: 41; Feb. 16: 22; Feb. 18: 26; Feb. 19: 34; Feb. 20: 34; Feb. 21: 41; Feb. 22: 34; Feb. 23: 22; Feb. 25: 29; Feb. 26: 35; Feb. 27: 30; Feb. 28: 61; Mar. 1: 45. ports. Newsp

67

George, Alexander R. Nothing like those other oldtime ceremonies: 4th term–but no fanfare. Washington post, Jan. 14, 1945: 6B. illus. Newsp

Briefly reviews some earlier inaugurals.

68

Gilbert, Clinton W. A part in the show. Collier's, v. 83, Mar. 9, 1929: 8-9, 48-49. illus. AP2.C65, v. 83

69

Gobright, Lawrence A. Recollection of men and things at Washington, during the third of a century. Philadelphia, Claxton, Remsen & Haffelfinger, 1869. 420 p. F198.G57

The following inaugurations are briefly described: Van Buren, p. 26-27; W. H. Harrison, p. 40-43; Polk, p. 69-70; Taylor, p. 97-99; Fillmore, p. 110; Pierce, p. 133; Buchanan, p. 166-167; Lincoln's first, p. 287-290; his second, p. 341-344; A. Johnson, p. 357.

70

Graham, Alberta P., *and* Muriel Fuller. Inaugural "firsts." American mercury, v. 60, Feb. 1945: 169-173. AP2.A37, v. 60

71

Green, Constance (McLaughlin). Washington. Princeton, N.J., Princeton University Press, 1962-63. 2 v. illus. F194.G7

Contents. v. 1. Village and Capital, 1800-1878. v. 2. Capital City, 1879-1950.

See index under names of Presidents.

72

Greeted like a king–irrepressible enthusiasm for the first President. Washington post, Mar. 5, 1905, pictorial souvenir section: 4. Newsp

Reviews some early inaugurations.

73

Griffiths, Harriet. They really loved a parade. Sunday, the star magazine (Washington), Jan. 15, 1961: 16-17. illus. Newsp

74

Grupp, George W. God and Presidential inaugurations. National republic, v. 44, Jan. 1957: 15-16, 31. ports. E171.N32, v. 44

75

Gwertzman, Bernard. U.S. inaugural agency urged. Sunday star (Washington), Jan. 22, 1961: A-1, A-8. Newsp

76

Hager, Alice R. Glamorous pageant of our inaugurals. From Washington's day on, they have touched the heart of the Nation. New York times magazine, Feb. 26, 1933: 8-9, 18. illus. AP2.N6575, 1933

77

Hale, William B. Presidential inaugurations at four crises: the scenes that attended the swearing-in of Washington, Jefferson, and Lincoln recalled–how Wilson will take the oath of office. World's work, v. 25, Mar. 1913: 508-514. AP2.W8, v. 25

78

Half a score of memorable Presidential inaugurations. Leslie's weekly, v. 108, Mar. 4, 1909: 204-205. AP2.L52, v. 108

Illustrations and captions only; no other text.

79

Halsey, Edwin A. Procedure and protocol of Presidential inaugurals. American Bar Association journal, v. 27, Jan. 1941: 17-22. illus. LL

80

Harvey, Charles M. Historic Presidential inaugurations. Leslie's weekly, v. 92, Mar. 2, 1901: 198-199. illus. AP2.L52, v. 92

Other illustrations on p. 196, 197.

81

Harvey, Charles M. Some of the most memorable Presidential inaugurations. Leslie's weekly, v. 100, Mar. 2, 1905: 198-199, 210. illus. AP2.L52, v. 100

82

Hazelton, George C. The National Capitol, its architecture, art, and history. New York, J. F. Taylor, 1903. 301 p. illus. F204.C2H43

Inaugurations: p. 80-84. Additional information is given on p. 144-145 (Jefferson), p. 161 (Arthur), p. 220 (Madison, Monroe, and Fillmore), and p. 239-240 (McKinley's second).

83

Helm, Edith (Benham). The captains and the kings. New York, Putnam [1954] 307 p. illus. E176.1.H44 1954

F. D. Roosevelt's fourth inauguration: p. 240-244.
Truman's second inauguration reception: p. 266-269.

84
Henry, John C. Good will of Nation put into pageant. Evening star (Washington), Jan. 20, 1937, inaugural ed.: 8-9. illus. Newsp

85
Henry, Laurin L. Presidential transitions. Washington, Brookings Institution [1960] xviii, 755 p. E743.H4

Wilson's first inauguration: p. 68-72.
Harding's inauguration: p. 196-200.
F. D. Roosevelt's first inauguration: p. 355-358.
Eisenhower's first inauguration: p. 529-531.

86
Henry, Thomas R. Inaugurations in the Star cover nearly a century. Evening star (Washington), Jan. 20, 1941, inaugural suppl.: 14-16. illus. Newsp

87
Henry, Thomas R. The pageant of past inaugurations. Sunday star (Washington), Mar. 5, 1933, pt. 7: 14-15. illus. Newsp

88
Henry, Thomas R. The parade of Presidents, 1801-1937. Evening star (Washington), Jan. 20, 1937, inaugural ed.: 16-17. illus. Newsp

89
Henry, Thomas R. Triumphal pageant of progress recorded by inaugurations. Evening star (Washington), Mar. 4, 1929, special inaugural section: 1, 7. illus. Newsp

90
Hill, William. Telling the story of inaugurations. Sunday star (Washington), Mar. 5, 1933, pt. 7: 28, 41. illus. Newsp

Newspaper coverage through the years.

91
Historic inaugurations. Frank Leslie's illustrated newspaper, v. 68, Mar. 9, 1889: 54. AP2.L52, v. 68

92
Hollander, Herbert S. Inaugurations form colorful pageant in annals of Nation. From beginning citizens have made occasion distinctly and

characteristically American; essence and basic trappings of inauguration day but little altered by time. Federal news, v. 2, Mar. 4, 1933: 1, 3. JK671.F4, v. 2

Includes a quiz on inaugurations.

93

Horan, James D. Mathew Brady, historian with a camera. Picture collation by Gertrude Horan. New York, Crown Publishers [1955] xix, 244 p. illus., map, ports. TR140.B7H6

Lincoln's second inauguration: plates 293, 306.
Grant's first inauguration: plate 357.
McKinley's inaugural parade (1897?): plate 419.

94

How they took the oath. Washington post, Mar. 4, 1893: 10. Newsp

95

Hurja, Emil Edward. History of Presidential inaugurations. With foreword by James A. Farley. New York, New York Democrat Pub. Corp., 1933. 62 p. JK536.H8

96

Hutchins, Stilson, *and* Joseph W. Moore. The National Capital, past and present; the story of its settlement, progress, and development. Washington, Post Pub. Co., 1885. 351 p. illus. F199.H97

Inaugurations: p. 266-285.

97

Hyman, Sidney. Oath leaves lot of leeway to conscience of President. Washington post, Jan. 21, 1957: C-1. Newsp

98

Inaugural attendance mark claimed by colored man, 80. Evening star (Washington), Jan. 11, 1937: B-1. port. Newsp

Charles H. Turner has seen every inauguration since President Grant's.

99

Inaugural ceremonies marked by series of "ups and downs." Evening star (Washington), Mar. 5, 1925: 34, 37. Newsp

100
Inaugural day made holiday. Washington post, Jan. 12, 1957: A-3.
Newsp

New legislation makes the day a legal holiday henceforth in the Washington metropolitan area.

101
Inaugural medals began in 1901. Evening star (Washington), Jan. 21, 1957, inaugural souvenir section: 19. illus. Newsp

102
Inaugural oath of office has been administered four times outside of the city of Washington. Sunday star (Washington), Feb. 28, 1909, pt. 4: 4. illus. Newsp

103
The 'inaugural pageant' through calm and crisis. Sunday star (Washington), Jan. 19, 1941, gravure section: 4-5. illus. Newsp

104
Inaugural show changing; in the long line of Presidents each term has started off with its own keynote. New York times, Jan. 19, 1941: 6E. illus. Newsp

Picture shows Jefferson dismounting from his horse to attend his inauguration in 1801.

105
Inauguration notes. United States law review, v. 67, Feb. 1933: 55-58.
LL

106
Inauguration of Warren G. Harding as President of the United States marks beginning of fourth big epoch in history of our country. Sunday star (Washington), Feb. 27, 1921, pt. 4: 1. illus. Newsp

Reviews earlier inaugurations.

107
Inauguration snapshots. Washingtonian, Mar. 1929: 24-25.
F191.W39, 1929

Scenes from the inaugurations of Wilson (1913), Harding, and Coolidge (1925).

108

Inaugurations are no novelty to retired D.C. physician, 88. Sunday star (Washington), Jan. 19, 1941, pt. 1: 9. port. Newsp

Dr. W. P. C. Hazen will watch his 14th inauguration.

109

Inaugurations at Washington. Harper's weekly, v. 41, Mar. 13, 1897: 250-251. AP2.H32, v. 41

110

Inaugurations of the past; some of the dramatic and picturesque circumstances under which Mr. Wilson's predecessors have been inducted into office. Harper's weekly, v. 57, Mar. 8, 1913: 14. AP2.H32, v. 57

Illustrations on p. 15-17 and 21.

111

Incidents of Presidential inaugurations. World's work, v. 1, Mar. 1901: 477-479. AP2.W8, v. 1

112

Jeffries, Ona G. In and out of the White House, from Washington to the Eisenhowers; an intimate glimpse into the social and domestic aspects of the Presidential life. New York, W. Funk [1960] 404 p. illus. E176.1.J4

Chronologically arranged, one chapter for each President. Information on inaugurations is given in many but not all cases.

Some information on inaugural balls; *see* index.

113

Jersey City. Free Public Library. Presidential inaugurations. [Jersey City, 1913] 11 p. JK536.J4

Compiled by Edmund W. Miller, assistant librarian.

114

Johnson, Gerald W. Nine inaugurations, nine turning points. New York times magazine, Jan. 18, 1953: 8-9, 40. illus. AP2.N6575, 1953

115

Jonas, Jack. The Rambler: our inaugurations just kept growing. Evening star (Washington), Dec. 13, 1956: B-1. Newsp

116

Jones, Dorothea, *and* Stuart E. Jones. Pennsylvania Avenue, route of Presidents. Landmarks and shrines of United States history line the path of inaugural parades from Capitol to White House. National geographic magazine, v. 111, Jan. 1957: 63-95. illus.

G1.N27, v. 111

117

Kane, Joseph N. Facts about the Presidents; a compilation of biographical and historical data. 2d ed. New York, H. W. Wilson Co., 1968. 384 p. ports.

E176.1.K3 1968

In the first part, which contains biographical data for the individual Presidents in their chronological order, each inauguration is briefly described. Statistical and comparative data, with miscellaneous information pertaining to inaugurals (such as Sunday inaugural dates, sites, weather, and the number of words in inaugural addresses), are supplied in the second part.

118

Kellogg, George T., *ed.* The inaugurations of all the United States Presidents, George Washington to Lyndon B. Johnson. [Washington, Colortone Press, 1965?] [37] p. illus.

JK536.K4

119

Kittler, Glenn D. Hail to the Chief! The inauguration days of our Presidents. Philadelphia, Chilton Books [1965] 242 p. illus., ports.

E176.1.K55

Bibliography: p. 232-235.

120

Klapthor, Margaret (Brown). The dresses of the First Ladies of the White House, as exhibited in the United States National Museum. Washington, Smithsonian Institution, 1952. 149 p. illus. (part col.) (Smithsonian Institution. Publication 4060)

GT605.K55

----- -----Supplement. The gown of Mrs. Harry S. Truman, as displayed in the United States National Museum, Smithsonian Institution. [Washington] Smithsonian Institution, 1954. [5] p. col. illus.

GT605.K55 Suppl.

----- -----Supplement. The gown of Mrs. Dwight D. Eisenhower, as displayed in the United States National Museum, Smithsonian Institution. [Washington] Smithsonian Institution, 1958. [5] p. col. illus.

GT605.K55 Suppl. 2

----- -----Supplement. The gown of Mrs. John F. Kennedy, as displayed in the United States National Museum, Smithsonian Institution. [Washington] Smithsonian Institution, 1963. [5] p. col. illus.
GT605.K55 Suppl. 3

Some of the gowns were worn at inaugural ceremonies.

121

Lack of Capitol space is inaugural problem. Evening star (Washington), Mar. 4, 1929, special inaugural section: 6. Newsp

122

Lawrence, David. Today in Washington: Nation found in need of law on Presidential oathtaking. New York herald-tribune, Jan. 23, 1953: 15. Newsp

123

Lawrence, Henry W. Recalling the strangest inaugurations. Sunday star (Washington), Feb. 26, 1933, pt. 7: 5. illus. Newsp

124

Lippincott, Sara J. (Clarke). A few inaugurations. Independent, v. 49, Feb. 25, 1897: 233-235. AP2.I53, v. 49

125

Lockwood, Mary (Smith). Historic homes in Washington; its noted men and women. New York, Belford Co. [c1889] 304 p. illus. F195.L79

Includes brief descriptions of the following inaugurations: J. Q. Adams, p. 74-75; Jackson's first, p. 77; Van Buren, p. 85-86, W. H. Harrison, p. 91; Pierce, p. 117; Lincoln's second, p. 122-124; Grant's first, p. 127-130; his second, p. 132; Garfield, p. 137-139.

126

Lockwood, Mary (Smith). Yesterdays in Washington. Rosslyn, Va., Commonwealth Co. [1915] 2 v. F194.L8

The following inaugurations are described in v. 1: Washington's first, p. 14-19; his second, p. 23-24; J. Adams, p. 68; Jefferson's first, p. 76-77, 87; Madison's first, p. 101-102; Monroe's first, p. 127-128; J. Q. Adams, p. 153-155; Jackson's first, p. 164-165; Van Buren, p. 190-191; W. H. Harrison, p. 200-202; Tyler, p. 209; Polk, p. 218-219; Taylor, p. 224-226; Pierce, p. 234-236; Buchanan, p. 242-244;

Lincoln's first, p. 261-265; his second, p. 272; A. Johnson, p. 274; Grant's first, p. 286-291; his second, p. 296-300; Hayes, p. 304-306; Cleveland's first, p. 321-322; B. Harrison, p. 324-325; McKinley's first, p. 336-338; his second, p. 343-349.

127

Logan, Mary S. (Cunningham). Thirty years in Washington; or, Life and scenes in our National Capital. With sketches of the Presidents and their wives ... from Washington's to Roosevelt's administration. Hartford, Conn., A. D. Worthington [c1905] xxxii, 752 p. illus.

F194.L82

Inauguration ceremonies: p. 162-171.

128

Lomask, Milton. "I do solemnly swear ..."; the story of the Presidential inauguration. New York, Ariel Books, Farrar, Straus & Giroux [1966] 175 p. F196.L62

Bibliography: p. [171]-175.

129

Longworth, Alice (Roosevelt). Crowded hours, reminiscences. New York, C. Scribner's Sons, 1933. 355 p. facsims., plates, ports.

E748.L87L8

Brief accounts of the following inaugurations: McKinley's second, p. 35-38; T. Roosevelt's second, p. 66-67; Taft, p. 165-166.

130

Lorant, Stefan. His Rough Riders featured with Teddy Roosevelt. Times-herald (Washington), Jan. 20, 1949: 6, 19. Newsp

Contrasts the inaugural ceremonies of the two Roosevelts.

131

Lorant, Stefan. Inaugurals trying for generals. Washington post, Jan. 20, 1953, special inaugural section: 2. illus. Newsp

132

Lorant, Stefan. The life and times of Theodore Roosevelt. Garden City, N.Y., Doubleday [1959] 640 p. illus., facsims., ports. E757.L85

Lincoln's inaugurations: p. 32, [40]-41.
T. Roosevelt's inaugurations: p. 357, 364, 420-[422].

Taft's inauguration: p. 506-[507].
Wilson's first inauguration: p. [582]-584.

133
Lorant, Stefan. The Presidency; a pictorial history of Presidential elections from Washington to Truman. New York, Macmillan, 1951. 755 p. illus. E183.L65

Includes some material on most of the inaugurations.

134
Low, A. Maurice. Democracy at its best; the power of the people is strikingly exemplified when the Presidency changes hands. Harper's weekly, v. 57, Mar. 22, 1913: 10. AP2.H32, v. 57

135
MacArthur, Harry. Eisenhower only the fifth to broadcast inaugural. Evening star (Washington), Jan. 20, 1953: B-17. Newsp

136
McGarraghy, Joseph C. Inaugural medals developed from identification badges. Evening star (Washington), Jan. 19, 1953: A-8. illus. Newsp

137
McKee, Thomas H. Presidential inaugurations from George Washington, 1789, to Grover Cleveland, 1893. With inaugural addresses complete. Washington, Statistical Pub. Co., 1893. 166 p. illus. JK536.M2

138
Marks, Dorothy. Inaugural faux pas started early. Diplomat, v. 12, Feb. 1961: 18, 63. illus. AP2.D575, v. 12

139
Mason, Guy. Our Presidents—how they have come and gone. Leslie's illustrated weekly newspaper, v. 116, Mar. 6, 1913: 244, 254. illus. AP2.L52, v. 116

140
Mayo, Earl W. The growth of the inaugural as a celebration. Harper's weekly, v. 45, Mar. 9, 1901: 256. illus. AP2.H32, v. 45

141

Merrill, L. T. Presidential inaugurations–old and new. Current history, v. 29, Mar. 1929: 905-911. illus. D410.C8, v. 29

142

Milhollen, Hirst D., *and* Milton Kaplan. Presidents on parade. New York, Macmillan Co., 1948. 425 p. illus., ports. E176.1.M63

Includes pictures of many inaugurations.

143

Miller, Hope R. Women accorded but meager roles in earlier inaugurations; first leaders' wives happy in background; eighteenth century newspapers failed to print the detailed accounts of social side of inaugural. Washington post, Jan. 20, 1937: B-11. ports. Newsp

144

Moore, Barbara. When Presidents take office. From Washington to Eisenhower, colorful twists and variations have attended the inauguration ceremony. American heritage, v. 4, spring 1953: 5-7. illus. E171.A43, v. 4

145

Morhart, Fred H. Collection of inaugural films sent to National Archives. Reels picture Presidential parades from McKinley to Coolidge. Evening star (Washington), Feb. 12, 1940: B-8. Newsp

146

Moyer, William J. Bigger and better parades for Presidents. Evening star (Washington), Jan. 20, 1953, special inaugural rotogravure section: 21. illus. Newsp

147

Moyer, William J. The girl who knew the Constituttion. Washington star pictorial magazine, Jan. 18, 1953: 28-29. illus. Newsp

Describes two occasions when the wording of the inaugural oath deviated from that prescribed by the Constitution (Taft, 1909; and Hoover, 1929, sworn in by Taft).

148

Moyer, William J. Too many Presidents as well as too few. Evening star (Washington), Jan. 20, 1953, special inaugural rotogravure section: 11. illus. Newsp

149

Murray, Mollie C. Inauguration traditions. Mayflower's log, Jan. 1941: 15, 26-27. F191.W39, 1941

150

The Nation comes to town and promptly goes on parade. Washington post Potomac, Jan. 17, 1965: 18, 20-21. illus. Newsp

151

National Geographic Society, *Washington, D.C.* Only United States has al fresco inauguration. Washington [1921] 4 l. (Geographic news bulletin, n.s., 371) G1.G32, n.s. 371

152

Nevins, Allan. The human side of inaugurations. American weekly, Jan. 18, 1953: 2. illus. AP2.A464, 1953

153

New York Association, *Washington, D.C.* Guide book of the inauguration of 1873, and historical sketch of previous inaugurations. New York Association. Presidential inauguration, March 4, 1873. [Washington, 1873] 28 p. F198.N58 Rare Bk. Coll.

"Historical Sketch of the Inauguration of the Presidents" [1789-1869]: p. [3]-13.

154

Nicolay, Helen. Our Capital on the Potomac. New York, Century Co. [1924] 545 p. illus. F194.N4

Includes accounts of inaugurations and inaugural balls of a number of the Presidents, particularly the earlier ones. *See* index under names of Presidents.

155

Noyes, Theodore W. Inauguration reminiscences. Text of T. W. Noyes' broadcast recalling ceremonies he has seen in last 50 years. Evening star (Washington), Jan. 20, 1941: B-1, B-6. port. Newsp

156

Oberdorfer, Don. No wonder Madison said, 'I'd rather be in bed.' New York times magazine, Jan. 17, 1965: 10-11, 28, 30, 33-34, 36, 38. illus. AP2.N6575, 1965

157

O'Malley, Frank W. Punching the White House time clock. Saturday evening post, v. 193, Feb. 26, 1921: 3-4, 62, 66, 69. illus.
AP2.S2, v. 193

158

Our eighteenth inauguration day. Harper's weekly, v. 1, Mar. 14, 1857: 168-170. illus. AP2.H32, v. 1

Describes earlier inaugurations.

159

Patterson, Bradley H. Inaugural! They're already getting the big ball ready to roll. Washington post Potomac, June 30, 1968: 11-12, 16. illus. Newsp

160

Pearson, Drew, *and* Robert S. Allen. Inaugurating the President. Redbook, v. 68, Feb. 1937: 15, 78-80. illus. AP2.R28, 1937

161

Pennypacker, Samuel W. Congress Hall: an address at the last session of the Court of Common Pleas, No. 2, in Congress Hall, Philadelphia, September sixteenth, MDCCCXCV. Philadelphia, Printed for the Philadelphia Bench and Bar, 1895. 34 p. F158.8.C7P4

Washington's second inauguration: p. 17-20.
Inauguration of John Adams: p. 21-24.

162

Pepper, Charles M. Every-day life in Washington, with pen and camera. New York, Christian Herald, 1900. 416 p. illus. F199.P42

The ceremony of inauguration: p. 62-75.
Oath-taking and inaugural addresses: p. 76-85.
Inaugural pomp and pageantry: p. 86-94.

163

Philp's Washington described. A complete view of the American Capital, and the District of Columbia. By William D. Haley. Washington, Philp & Solomons [1860?] 239 p. illus., map. F198.P564

Inaugurations: p. 76-82.

164

Poore, Benjamin Perley. Perley's reminiscences of sixty years in the national metropolis. Philadelphia, Hubbard Bros. [c1886] 2 v. illus., facsims., ports. F194.P822 Rare Bk. Coll.

Inauguration of J. Q. Adams, v. 1, p. 26-27; Jackson, p.93-95; Van Buren, p. 198-201; W. H. Harrison, p. 250-255; Tyler, p. 269-270; Polk, p. 326-328; Taylor, p. 353-355; Fillmore, p. 379; Pierce, p. 424-427; Buchanan, p. 513-516; Lincoln, v. 2, p. 68-71, 157-163; Johnson, p. 181; Grant, p. 249-253, 294-299; Hayes, p. 339-340; Garfield, p. 388-398; Arthur, p. 428-430; Cleveland, p. 483-489.

165

Poore, Benjamin Perley. Reminiscences of Washington. Atlantic monthly, v. 45, Jan., Mar.-Apr., June 1880: 53-66, 289-299, 537-548, 806-817; v. 46, July, Sept.-Dec. 1880: 67-75, 369-379, 531-542, 664-675, 799-810; v. 47, Feb., Apr.-May 1881: 234-250, 538-547, 658-666. AP2.A8, v. 45-47

Inauguration of J. Q. Adams, v. 45: 289; Van Buren, v. 46: 67-68; W. H. Harrison, v. 46: 369, 372-373; Tyler, v. 46: 531; Polk, v. 46: 799; Taylor, v. 47: 236-237; Fillmore, v. 47: 538.

166

Presidential inaugurals–1789-1929; a brief chronology of ceremonials from Washington to Hoover. Congressional digest, v. 8, Mar. 1929: 66-73, 96. JK1.C65, v. 8

167

Presidential inaugurations. Leslie's weekly, v. 92, Mar. 2, 1901: 194. AP2.L52, v. 92

168

The Presidents of the United States and the Baltimore and Ohio Railroad. Baltimore and Ohio employes magazine, v. 1, Mar. 1913: 1-3. illus. TF1.B3, v. 1

169

Previous Presidential inaugurations. Scenes and incidents attending the installation in office of the Chief Magistrates of the United States from Washington to Benjamin Harrison. New York herald, Mar. 5, 1893: 30-32. illus. Newsp

170
Proctor, John C. Inaugural programs with riotous accompaniments recalled. Sunday star (Washington), Nov. 25, 1928, pt. 7: 3. illus.
Newsp

About the inaugurations of Cleveland (1885) and Benjamin Harrison (1889).

171
Proctor, John C. Some highlights of early inaugurations in Washington. Sunday star (Washington), Jan. 6, 1952: C-2. Newsp

172
Proctor, John C. Spectacular features have been associated with some inaugural days. Sunday star (Washington), Jan. 19, 1941, pt. 2: 4. illus. Newsp

173
A quiz for inauguration day: who said it? Parade, Jan. 15, 1961: 2. illus.
AP2.P263, 1961

174
Reed, Joseph. Inaugurals of the past: simple, colorful, and dramatic. Washington post, Jan. 19, 1941: B2-B3. illus. Newsp

175
Ripley, Josephine. Inaugural: then and now. Truman ceremony adds to long history of color, drama, and national significance. Christian Science monitor magazine, Dec. 24, 1948: 2, 13. illus.
AP2.C5255, 1948

176
Roberts, Chalmers M. Out of the past; a page from history. Evening star (Washington), Jan. 20, 1949, special inaugural gravure section: 7. illus.
Newsp

177
Roberts, Chalmers M. Presidential inaugurations epitomize democracy. Washington post, Jan. 20, 1953, special inaugural section: 1, 6. illus. Newsp

325-882 O-69—3

178

Ross, Ishbel. Proud Kate, portrait of an ambitious woman. New York, Harper [c1953] 309 p. illus. E415.9.S76R6

Biography of Kate Chase Sprague.
Lincoln's inaugurations: p. 60-61, 167-169.
Grant's inaugurations: p. 211, 228.

179

Rubin, Theodore. Inauguration footnotes. Coronet, v. 25, Jan. 1949: 103. AP2.C767, 1949

180

Salamanca, Lucy. Political history recorded in American inaugurals. Sunday star (Washington), Jan. 17, 1937, pt. 4: 1, 8. illus. Newsp

181

Seaton, Josephine. William Winston Seaton of the "National intelligencer." A biographical sketch. Boston, J. R. Osgood, 1871. 385 p. PN4874.S4S4

Madison's second inauguration: p. 99.
Jackson's first inauguration: p. 210-212.

182

Sevareid, Arnold Eric. Small sounds in the night; a collection of capsule commentaries on the American scene. New York, Knopf, 1956. 305 p. E835.S4

"None but the Honest and Wise": p. 57-59.
"Continuity's Conquest": p. 60-62.
Broadcast over CBS on Jan. 19 and 20, 1953; the first discusses inaugurals in general and the second, Eisenhower's first inauguration.

183

Simplicity marked many inaugurations of the past. Sunday star (Washington), Mar. 4, 1917, pt. 4: 2. illus. Newsp

184

Singleton, Esther. The story of the White House. New York, McClure Co., 1907. 2 v. F204.W5S6

Contains scattered information on inaugurations and inaugural balls. *See* index.

185
Smith, Don. Peculiarities of the Presidents; strange and intimate facts not found in history. [4th ed. Van Wert, Ohio, 1947, c1946] 185 p. illus. E176.1.S647 1947

Inaugurals: p. 34-43.

186
Smith, Margaret (Bayard). The first forty years of Washington society, portrayed by the family letters of Mrs. Samuel Harrison Smith (Margaret Bayard) from the collection of her grandson, J. Henley Smith; edited by Gaillard Hunt. New York, C. Scribner's Sons, 1906. 424 p. facsims., plates, ports. F194.S65

Jefferson's first inauguration: p. 25-26.
Madison's first inauguration and inaugural ball: p. 58-59, 61-62, 410-412.
Jackson's first inauguration: p. 290-297.

187
Smithsonian Institution. The First Ladies Hall, Smithsonian Institution. [Text by Margaret W. Brown Klapthor] Washington, 1965. [16] p. illus. (*Its* Publication, 4640) GT605.S55 1965

Some of the gowns described were worn at inaugural ceremonies.

188
Some inaugurals of early times. Evening star (Washington), Mar. 4, 1909, pt. 3: 1-2. Newsp

189
Spiegelman, Julia. Changing styles in inaugurations. Christian Science monitor weekly magazine, Jan. 6, 1945: 3. illus. AP2.C5255, 1945

190
Steinberg, Alfred. 'Little things' of 40 inaugurals make up traditions of the day. Washington post, Dec. 26, 1948: 3B. illus. Newsp

191
Stevenson, Victoria F. Inaugurations differ widely in their ceremonial character. Sunday star (Washington), Mar. 1, 1925, pt. 5: 3, 6. illus. Newsp

192

Stevenson, Victoria F. Presidents who drove to Washington to be inaugurated. American motorist, v. 7, Mar. 1933: 6-7, 35. illus.

TL1.A465, v. 7

193

Stewart, Jay. Inaugurating a President; interesting yet simple ceremonies by which the President of the United States assumes his office. New England home magazine, v. 14, Mar. 3, 1901: 18-19, 22.

AP2.N3775, v. 14

Illustrations of scenes at an earlier inauguration (1897?) appear on p. 8, 17, 20, 21.

194

Talking about inaugurations ... United States news, v. 10, Jan. 24, 1941: 9. illus.

JK1.U65, v. 10

Brief notes on 12 inaugurations from 1865 to 1941.

195

Tarver, William S. Where thousands watch big parade. Sunday star (Washington), Mar. 5, 1933, pt. 7: 40. illus.

Newsp

On the construction of grandstands.

196

Thomas, Gene. U.S. inaugurations always reflect current aims of Nation. Sunday star (Washington), Mar. 1, 1925, pt. 5: 1. illus.

Newsp

197

Tindall, William. Standard history of the city of Washington from a study of the original sources. Knoxville, Tenn., H. W. Crew, 1914. 600 p. illus.

F194.T64

Brief information on the inaugurations of the Presidents from Jefferson to Wilson. *See* index.

198

"To preserve, protect, and defend the Constitution"; the inaugurations of the first nine Presidents of the United States are a story of quainter customs and simpler manners than those of our day. Our world weekly, v. 2, Mar. 2, 1925: 70-71, 78; Mar. 9: 90, 94. illus.

AP2.O78, v. 2

199

Today's inaugural scores 'first.' Evening star (Washington), Jan. 20, 1961: AA-24. Newsp

Lists 24 other inaugural "firsts" from Washington to Eisenhower.

200

Todd, Charles B. The story of Washington, the National Capital. New York, G. P. Putnam's Sons, 1889. xviii, 416 p. illus., facsims., map, plan. (Great cities of the Republic, [v. 2]) F194.T68

The following inaugurations are briefly described: Jefferson's first, p. 54-56; Madison's first, p. 67; his second, p. 381; Lincoln's first, p. 135-138; Cleveland's first, p. 178-179.

201

Truett, Randle B. The First Ladies in fashion. With fashion notes by Philip Robertson. New York, Hastings House [1965, c1954] 84 p. illus. GT605.T7 1965

Some of the gowns described were worn at inaugural ceremonies.

202

U.S. *Library of Congress.* Presidential inaugurations of past are theme of new exhibition at the Library of Congress. Washington [1945] 2 l. (*Its* Press release no. 227) Z663.A45,1945

203

U.S. *National Archives.* List of motion pictures and sound recordings relating to Presidential inaugurations, compiled by E. Daniel Potts. Washington, 1960. 20 p. (*Its* Publication no. 61-5. Special lists, no. 16) F196.U5

204

U.S. *National Archives.* Preliminary inventory of the records of inaugural committees (Record group 274) Compiled by Hardee Allen. Washington, 1960. 45 p. (*Its* Publication no. 61-8. Preliminary inventories, no. 131) CD3026.A32, no. 131

205

U.S. *National Archives.* Preliminary inventory of the records of the 1961 Inaugural Committee (Record group 274) Compiled by Marion M.

Johnson. Washington, 1964. 18 p. (*Its* Publication no. 65-5. Preliminary inventories, no. 162) CD3026.A32, no. 162

206

Van Rensselaer, May (King), *and* Frederic F. Van de Water. The social ladder. New York, H. Holt, 1924. 309 p. illus. F128.37.V27

Washington society and the inaugural festivities: p. 253-258.

207

Washington, D.C. Inaugural Committee, *1885.* Official programme of the inauguration ceremonies of Hon. Grover Cleveland and Hon. Thomas A. Hendricks, as President and Vice President of the United States, Washington, D.C., March 5th, 1885. New York, J. T. Cowdery, 1885. [48] p. illus., map, ports. DWP

"History of Former Inaugurations," by A. C. Wheeler: p. [15]-[23]. In Cleveland 1885 folder.

208

Washington, D.C. Inaugural Committee, *1901.* Inaugural souvenir, 1901. [Washington, Press of W. F. Roberts, 1901] 22 l. illus. F199.W31 1901I

Contains brief descriptions of earlier inaugural ceremonies, from Washington's first through McKinley's first.

209

Washington, D.C. Inaugural Committee, *1949.* Records in the National Archives pertaining to Presidential inaugural ceremonies and related activities, 1861-1945. [Washington, 1949] 4 l. (*Its* Mimeo, no. 112) DWP

In Truman inauguration scrapbook.

210

Washington drama: three crucial inaugurals. New York times magazine, Jan. 15, 1961: 7. illus. AP2.N6575, 1961

Scenes from the swearing in of F. D. Roosevelt, 1933; Truman, 1945; and Eisenhower, 1957.

211

We love a parade. Mayflower's log, Jan. 1937: 8-10. illus. F191.W39, 1937

212

When inaugurals were 'photographed' in ink. Times-herald (Washington), Dec. 1, 1940: C-3. illus. Newsp

213

When March 4, "Inauguration Day," falls on a Sunday. Sunday star (Washington), Mar. 4, 1917, pt. 4: 1. illus. Newsp

214

White, William S. Washington in inauguration time: behind carnival aspects are those who see a grand passage. Evening star (Washington), Jan. 18, 1961: A-17. Newsp

215

Wilbur, Harriette. Inauguration days. St. Nicholas, v. 48, Mar. 1921: 396-405. illus. AP201.S3, v. 48

216

Williamson, S. T. Washington's one day of days. New York times magazine, Mar. 3, 1929: 1-2, 16. illus. Newsp

217

Wilson, Frederick T. Our most unusual Presidential inaugurations. Extension of remarks of Hon. Chapman Revercomb, of West Virginia, in the Senate of the United States, Wednesday, February 20, 1957. Congressional record, 85th Congress, 1st session, v. 103: A1261-A1262. J11.R5, v. 103

218

Wilson, Rufus R. Washington, the Capital City, and its part in the history of the Nation. Philadelphia, J. B. Lippincott Co., 1901. 2 v. plates. F194.W75

Includes brief descriptions of inaugurations from Jefferson through Grant, with the exception of Tyler.

INAUGURAL ADDRESSES (Collective)

219

Austen, Albert A. The "traditional" Presidential inaugural address. *In* Kirk, Rudolf, *and* Charles F. Main, *eds.* Essays in literary history presented to J. Milton French. New Brunswick, N.J., Rutgers University Press [1960] p. [239]-248. PR14.K5

220

Gross, Gerald C. Inaugural talks have been customary since Washington's day. Washington post, Jan. 20, 1937: 2-B, 10-B. illus. Newsp

221

Owsley, Clifford D. Inaugural. [New York] Olympic Press [c1964] 154 p. J81.C64

"Originated as a master's thesis at the American University, Washington, D.C."

Bibliography: p. 152-154.

222

Smylie, James H. Providence and Presidents; types of American piety in Presidential inaugurals. Religion in life, v. 35, spring 1966: 270-282. BR1.R28, v. 35

223

U.S. *President.* The Chief Executive; inaugural addresses of the Presidents of the United States, from George Washington to Lyndon B. Johnson. With an introduction by Arthur Schlesinger, Jr., and commentary by Fred L. Israel. Conceived and edited by Chelsea House Publishers. New York, Crown Publishers [1965] 312 p. ports. J81.C65

224

U.S. *President.* The inaugural addresses of the American Presidents, from Washington to Kennedy. Annotated by Davis Newton Lott. New York, Holt, Rinehart, and Winston [1961] 299 p. illus. J81.C61

225

U.S. *President.* The inaugural addresses of the Presidents; containing the inaugural address of every elected President from Washington to Hoover, with biographical sketches and a prefatory comment by the compiler. Compiled and edited by Renzo D. Bowers. St. Louis, Mo., Thomas Law Book Co., 1929. 461 p. J81.C29

226

U.S. *President.* Inaugural addresses of the Presidents of the United States. Edited by John Vance Cheney. [2d ed.] Chicago, Reilly & Britton Co., 1906. 2 v. fronts. (The Patriotic classics) J81.C06a

Contents. [v. 1] From Washington to Polk. [v. 2] From Taylor to Roosevelt.

227

U.S. *President.* Inaugural addresses of the Presidents of the United States from George Washington, 1789, to Harry S. Truman, 1949. [Washington, U.S. Govt. Print. Off., 1952] 244 p. (82d Congress, 2d session. House document no. 540) J81.C49

"Compiled from research volumes and State papers by the Legislative Reference Service, Library of Congress."

228

U.S. *President.* Inaugural addresses of the Presidents of the United States from George Washington, 1789, to John F. Kennedy, 1961. Washington, U.S. Govt. Print. Off., 1961. 270 p. ports. (87th Congress, 1st session. House document no. 218) J81.C61a

"Compiled from research volumes and State papers by the Legislative Reference Service, Library of Congress."

229

U.S. *President.* Inaugural addresses of the Presidents of the United States from George Washington, 1789, to Lyndon Baines Johnson, 1965. Washington, U.S. Govt. Print. Off., 1965. 274 p. (89th Congress, 1st session. House document no. 51) J81.C65a

"Compiled from research volumes and State papers by the Legislative Reference Service, Library of Congress."

230

U.S. *President.* Inaugural addresses of the Presidents of the United States from Johnson to Roosevelt. Edited by John Vance Cheney. Chicago, R. R. Donnelley, 1905. 125 p. front. (The Lakeside classics) J81.C05

231

U.S. *President.* Presidential inaugurals, 1789-1897. [Providence? J. W. Kerwin, 1897?] 56 p. illus. JK536.A5 1897

Inaugural addresses, Washington to McKinley.

232

U.S. *President.* The Presidents speak; the inaugural addresses of the American Presidents from Washington to Kennedy. Annotated by Davis Newton Lott. New York, Holt, Rinehart and Winston [1962, c1961] 299 p. illus. J81.C62

233

U.S. *President, 1789-1797 (Washington)* The inaugural speeches of Washington, Adams and Jefferson. [Boston] Printed by H. Sprague, 1802. 40 p. E310.U58 Rare Bk. Coll.

234

Wolfarth, Donald L. The inaugural addresses of the Presidents of the United States: a content analysis. Ann Arbor, Mich., University Microfilms [1959] Micro AC-1, no. 59-6048

Microfilm copy (positive) of typescript.

Collation of the original, as determined from the film: x, 292 l. tables.

Thesis–University of Minnesota.

Abstracted in *Dissertation Abstracts,* v. 20, Dec. 1959, p. 2443.

Bibliography: leaves 285-292.

INAUGURAL BALLS

235

Ames, Mary (Clemmer). A woman's letter from Washington–the inauguration ball. Independent, v. 25, Mar. 20, 1873: 358-359. AP2.I53, v. 25

236

Ball. New Yorker, v. 24, Jan. 29, 1949: 19. AP2.N6763, v. 24

237

The ball room building. A magnificent ball-room. Features of the great ball. The program of the ball. Regulations for the ball. Evening star (Washington), Mar. 3, 1885: 3. illus. Newsp

238

Balls of former days; festivities attending the Presidential inauguration. Evening star (Washington), Mar. 3, 1885: 3. Newsp

239

Barbee, David R. Dance units backed inauguration balls; Madison's, in 1809, first of its kind; Grant's held in zero weather. *In* The Washington post. Inaugural edition, Saturday, March 4, 1933. Washington, 1933. p. 4. E806.W28

240
Barbee, David R. Lincoln leaves second ball when dancers mob supper. *In* The Washington post. Inaugural edition, Saturday, March 4, 1933. Washington, 1933. p. 15. E806.W28

241
Barbee, David R. Washington danced at first inaugural; event in June, 1789, delayed by belated arrival of President's wife. *In* The Washington post. Inaugural edition, Saturday, March 4, 1933. Washington, 1933. p. 14. E806.W28

242
Beale, Betty. Some pros and cons on inaugural balls. Sunday star (Washington), Nov. 18, 1956: D-1, D-14. illus. Newsp

243
Bliss, Louis D. The electrical features of the inaugural ball. American electrician, v. 9, Mar. 1897: 77-79. illus. TK1.A4, v. 9

244
Campbell, Jennie S. Inaugural balls of the past. National magazine, v. 13, Mar. 1901: 441-446. illus. AP2.N34, v. 13

245
Canby, Margaret H. Armory to bloom with flowers; thousands of gardenias gift of Mexico for inaugural ball. Evening star (Washington), Jan. 14, 1949: B-3. Newsp

246
Cavanagh, Catherine F. Our inaugural balls. Delineator, v. 65, Mar. 1905: 516-519. TT500.D3, v. 65

247
Clark, Allen C. [First inaugural ball] *In* Columbia Historical Society, *Washington, D.C.* Records. v. 33/34; 1929-32. Washington, 1932. p. 302-303. F191.C72, v. 33/34

In his article, "The Mayoralty of Robert Brent."

The ball described was held at Long's Hotel on Mar. 4, 1809.

248
Coontz, John L. Gay memories of past inaugural balls. Sunday star (Washington), Mar. 5, 1933, pt. 7: 22-23. illus. Newsp

249

Crowninshield, Mary (Bradford). The inaugural ball at Washington. Delineator, v. 57, May 1901: 803-808. illus. TT500.D3, v. 57

250

Cullinane, James. Private inaugural balls replace Presidential functions. Washington post, Jan. 20, 1937: 10-B. Newsp

251

Ellet, Elizabeth F. (Lummis). The queens of American society. New York, C. Scribner, 1867. 464 p. ports. E176.E43

First inaugural ball (May 7, 1789): p. 24-25.
Madison's inaugural ball: p. 247.

252

Famous inaugural balls and receptions of the past. Sunday star (Washington), Jan. 23, 1921, pt. 4: 2. Newsp

253

First lady's finery; for the inaugural ball she chose pearls and glittery pink. Life, v. 34, Jan. 26, 1953: 77-78. illus. AP2.L547, v. 34

254

Grant, G. B. The inauguration ball, notable evening entertainment of the Government's birthday. New England home magazine, v. 14, Mar. 3, 1901: 23, 25-26. AP2.N3775, v. 14

255

The historic ball upon inauguration day. Harper's weekly, v. 53, Mar. 6, 1909: 29. AP2.H32, v. 53

256

History of inaugural balls dates back to Madison's day. Evening star (Washington), Mar. 3, 1925: 11. Newsp

257

History of inaugural balls revives question of perpetuation. Evening star (Washington), Mar. 4, 1929, special inaugural section: 5. illus. Newsp

258
Hughes, Carolyn B. The gala and the ball. Washington post Potomac, Jan. 17, 1965: 24, 26-27. illus. Newsp

259
Hunt, Gaillard. The first inauguration ball. Century magazine, v. 69, Mar. 1905: 754-760. ports. AP2.C4, v. 69

260
Hurd, Charles. Washington cavalcade. New York, E. P. Dutton, 1948. 320 p. F196.H8

Brief information on some inaugural balls; *see* index.

261
The inaugural ball; inaugural ball gowns. Washington capital, v. 20, Mar. 9, 1901: 7-8. F191.W27, v. 20

262
Inaugural ball plans recall historic entertainments of earlier days. Washington herald, Jan. 22, 1933: 3-C. Newsp

263
Inaugural balls of past century. Evening star (Washington), Mar. 4, 1909, pt. 3: 1-2. illus. Newsp

264
Inaugural jam. Life, v. 34, Feb. 16, 1953: 43. col. illus.
AP2.L547, v. 34

Scene at one of the balls.

265
Inauguration ball at Washington, on the 4th of March. Frank Leslie's illustrated newspaper, v. 11, Mar. 23, 1861: 285. AP2.L52, v. 11

Illustrations on p. 273, 276, 277.

266
The inauguration ball, from Madison to McKinley. Harper's weekly, v. 41, Mar. 13, 1897: 262. AP2.H32, v. 41

Grand ball in honor of the first inauguration of President Lincoln, held on March 4, 1861, in a hall especially erected for the occasion. From *Frank Leslie's Illustrated Newspaper*—see item 265.

267

Jonas, Jack. The Rambler: about the belle of another ball. Evening star (Washington), Jan. 21, 1957: A-21. Newsp

Describes the ball of Mar. 4, 1809.

268

Last official ball was held for the Tafts. Washington herald, Mar. 14, 1929: 28. Newsp

269

Long wait. New Yorker, v. 28, Jan. 31, 1953: 20-22. AP2.N6763, v. 28

270

McLendon, Winzola. Even in Madison's time, inaugural balls were a crush. Washington post, Jan. 17, 1965: F-7. illus. Newsp

271

McOmie, Margaret. At our President's first night. American motorist, v. 7, Feb. 1933: 4-5, 33, 40. illus. TL1.A465, v. 7

272

Men wore hats, ladies wraps for Grant's inaugural ball. Evening star (Washington), Mar. 5, 1925: 36. Newsp

Also gives information on some other past inaugural balls.

273

Mesta, Perle (Skirvin). Perle—my story, by Perle Mesta with Robert Cahn. New York, McGraw-Hill [1960] 251 p. illus. CT275.M498A3

Inaugural ball, 1949: p. 123-125.

274

Passing of the inaugural ball not a social loss. New York times, Jan. 26, 1913, magazine section: 2. illus. Newsp

275

Past inaugural balls. Washington post, Mar. 5, 1897, pt. 3: 4. Newsp

276

Reprise of the first inaugural ball. Life, v. 42, Mar. 18, 1957: 165-166. illus. AP2.L547, v. 42

Party given by the Franklin National Bank, Franklin Square, Long Island.

277

Revival of inaugural ball pleasing to Washington. Washington post, Dec. 26, 1920, features section: 1. port. Newsp

Reviews history of inaugural balls.

278

Ripley, Josephine. Keeping the Presidents up; an intimate message from Washington. Christian science monitor, Jan. 24, 1949: 14. Newsp

A brief description of President Truman's inaugural ball and some information on past inaugural balls.

279

The social climax of the inaugural. Mayflower's log, Mar. 1933: 17-18. F191.W39, 1933

280

10,000 make merry at last [official] inaugural ball in 1909. Washington post, Mar. 4, 1925, inaugural ed.: 2. Newsp

281

Thayer, Mary V. Inaugural ball Dolly's idea. Washington post, Nov. 18, 1956: F-1, F-22. Newsp

282

Thayer, Mary V. They danced in overcoats at icy 'Muslin Palace' for Grant's inaugural. Washington post, Jan. 14, 1949: 5C. Newsp

283

Washington, D.C. Inaugural Committee, *1933.* [The inaugural ball] Washington, 1933. 2 l. DWP

Press release.
In Inaugural Balls folder.

284
When they dined with Mr. Lincoln. American home, v. 57, Feb. 1957: 66. illus. NA7100.A45, v. 57

Bill of fare of the Presidential inauguration ball of Mar. 6, 1865.

285
White tie. New Yorker, v. 36, Jan. 28, 1961: 26-27. AP2.N6763, v. 36

286
Wood, Walter. Inaugural balls started in Dolly Madison's time. Evening star (Washington), Jan. 20, 1953, special inaugural rotogravure section: 15. illus. Newsp

Invitations, Programs, and Other Memorabilia

287
Inauguration ball ... 5th [of March, 1821] at Brown's Hotel. [Invitation and admission ticket] Washington, 1821. 1 p. Mss

In U.S. Miscellany, Executive Mansion.

288
Inauguration ball ... 4th of March [1825], at the Washington Assembly rooms. [Invitation. Washington, 1825] 1 p. Mss

In U.S. Miscellany, Executive Mansion.

289
Inauguration ball ... 4th of March [1829] at Carusi's. [Invitation. Washington, 1829] 1 p. port. Mss

In U.S. Miscellany, Executive Mansion.

290
1841 inauguration ball ... at the new Washington Assembly rooms. [Invitation] Philada., Underwood, Bald. Spencer & Hufty [1841] 1 p. port. Mss

In U.S. Miscellany, Executive Mansion (2 copies).
Another copy in Rare Bk. Coll., Broadside portfolio 232, no. 14.

291
Inauguration ball. At a meeting of the Managers on Monday evening, the 11th January, the following preliminary arrangements were adopted ... [Washington, 1841?] [2] l. Rare Bk. Coll.

Broadside portfolio 210, no. 34.

325-882 O-69—4

292
1849 national inauguration ball ... at the Washington Assembly Rooms, Jackson Hall. [Invitation. Washington, 1849] 1 p. port. Mss

In U.S. Miscellany, Executive Mansion.

293
Grand inauguration ball. March 5th, 1849. Judiciary Square. [Invitation. Washington, 1849] 1 p. illus. Mss

In U.S. Miscellany, Executive Mansion.

294
Grand national inauguration ball, Washington City, Judiciary Square, March fourth, 1857. [Invitation] Philada., Toppan, Carpenter [1857] 1 p. port. Mss

In U.S. Miscellany, Executive Mansion.
Copy also in DWP, in Buchanan folder.

295
Union ball, 1861 ... on Monday evening, March 4th, at Washington, D.C. [Invitation] Washington, Philp & Solomons [1861] 1 p. DWP

In Lincoln folder.

296
Inauguration ball, Monday evening, March 6, 1865. [Admission ticket for] one gentleman and two ladies. Washington [1865] 1 p.
Rare Bk. Coll.

Stern Collection, broadside portfolio 9, no. 43.

297
National inauguration ball, March 4th, 1865. [Invitation. Washington, 1865] 1 p. ports. Mss

In U.S. Miscellany, Executive Mansion (2 copies).

298
Grant. Colfax. March 4, 1869. Inauguration reception ... to be given at the United States Treasury Building at Washington, D.C., on the evening of March 4th, 1869. (Dancing) [Invitation] Washington, Philp & Solomons [1873] 1 p. illus. DWP

In Grant folder.

299

Inauguration ball, Washington, March 4, 1873. [Souvenir. Washington, 1873] [8] p. DWP

Includes lists of committee members and order of dancing.

In Grant folder.

300

[Invitation to] the inauguration ball on the evening of March 4th, 1873. [Washington, Philp & Solomons, 1873?] folder.

Rare Bk. Coll.

Text on p. [1].

Broadside portfolio 206, no. 36a.

301

Inauguration ball, March 4th, 1881. [Programme. New York, Kendall Bank Note Co., 1881] [12] p. col. illus., ports. Rare Bk. Coll.

Includes lists of committee members, program of promenade concert, and order of dancing.

Batchelder broadside portfolio 1, no. 4.

Three copies also in DWP, in Garfield folder.

302

Inauguration ball, March 4th, 1885. [Souvenir ticket] Washington, V. G. Fischer, 1885. 1 p. ports. DWP

Two copies in Cleveland 1885 folder.

303

Souvenir of the inauguration ball, March 4th, 1885. [Philadelphia, Engraved & printed for V. G. Fischer, Washington, D.C., by E. A. Wright, 1885] 16 p. illus., ports. Mss

Includes lists of committee members, program of promenade concert, order of dancing, and menu.

Accompanied by an admission ticket to the ball, held at the New Pension Building; a supper ticket; and a ticket to the promenade concert, held at the same place on Mar. 5.

In the Presidential Papers, Grover Cleveland, Series 9, subseries H.

Two copies of the souvenir only are also in DWP, Cleveland 1885 folder.

304

Program, inaugural ball, New Pension Building, March 4th, 1889. [Phila., Bailey, Banks & Biddle, 1889] [16] p. illus. DWP

Includes lists of committee members, order of dancing, and bill of fare.

Two copies in Benjamin Harrison folder.

305

Souvenir, inaugural ball, March 4th, 1889. [Phila., Bailey, Banks & Biddle, 1889] [3] l. plates (part col.), ports. Rare Bk. Coll.

Broadside portfolio 207, no. 41b.

Two copies also in DWP, in Benjamin Harrison folder.

306

Inaugural ball and reception, March 4, 1893. [Souvenir. Washington] Bureau of Engraving and Print. [1893] 1 p. ports. Mss

In U.S. Miscellany, Executive Mansion.

Two copies also in DWP, in Cleveland (undated) folder.

307

Inaugural ball, March 4th, 1893. New Pension Building. Pass [for] private carriage. [Washington, 1893] 1 p. DWP

In Cleveland 1893 folder.

308

[Inaugural ball, March fourth, 1893] Programme. [Phila., Bailey, Banks & Biddle, 1893] [15] p. DWP

Includes order of dancing, menu, and lists of committee members.

Two copies in Cleveland 1893 folder.

309

Inaugural ball, March 4th, 1897. [Souvenir] Philadelphia, Bailey Banks & Biddle Co. [1897] [3] l. illus. (part col.), ports. Mss

In U.S. Miscellany, Executive Mansion.

A copy also in Rare Bk. Coll.

310

McKinley Hobart inaugural ball. Phila., Bailey Banks & Biddle Co. [1897] 12 p. ports. Mss

In silk cover.

Includes lists of committee members, program of promenade concert, order of dancing, and bill of fare.

In U.S. Miscellany, Executive Mansion.

Copy (without silk cover) also in DWP, in McKinley folder.

311

March 4th, 1897, inaugural supper [admission ticket] Phila., Bailey Banks & Biddle Co. [1897] 1 p. DWP

In McKinley folder.

312

Regulations, inaugural ball, March 4, 1897, Pension Office, Judiciary Square, Washington, D.C. Washington, Gibson Bros., Prs. [1897] [4] p. plans. Rare Bk. Coll.

Broadside portfolio 207, no. 57.

313

Inaugural ball, Pension Building, March fourth, 1901. [Admission ticket. Washington, 1901] DWP

In McKinley folder.

314

March fourth, 1901, inaugural ball. [Program. Washington, 1901] 12 p. Rare Bk. Coll.

Includes lists of committee members, program of promenade concert, order of dancing, and menu.

Two copies in Batchelder broadside portfolio 1, no. 9.

Copy also in DWP, in McKinley folder.

315

Menu, inaugural ball supper, March 4th, 1901. [Washington?] Press of B. S. Adams [1901] [4] p. illus., ports. DWP

In McKinley folder.

316

Inaugural ball, March fourth, 1905. [Program. Washington, W. F. Roberts Co., 1905] 15 p. DWP

Includes program of promenade music, lists of committee members, order of dancing, and menu.

In Theodore Roosevelt folder.

317

Inaugural ball, March fourth, 1909. Pension Building. [Admission ticket. Washington, 1909] 1 p. DWP

In Taft folder.

318

Inaugural ball, March fourth, 1909. [Program. Washington? 1909] [4] p. DWP

Includes program of promenade concert, order of dancing, and menu.

In Taft folder.

319

Souvenir program, charity inaugural ball, March 4, 1925, the Mayflower Hotel, Washington, D.C. [Washington, H-K Advertising Service, 1925] [36] p. illus., ports. P&P

In Presidential file–Coolidge.

320

[Invitation to] the inaugural ball, Thursday evening, the twentieth of January, one thousand nine hundred and forty-nine, at ten o'clock, National Guard Armory, Washington. [Washington, 1949] 1 p. DWP

In Truman inauguration scrapbook.

BIBLES

321

Barbee, David R. McKinley took oath on beautiful Bible. *In* The Washington post. Inaugural edition, Saturday, March 4, 1933. Washington, 1933. p. 18. E806.W28

322

The Bible holder. Newsweek, v. 25, Jan. 29, 1945: 41. illus. AP2.N6772, v. 25

323

Bible on which Wilson may take oath. Washington post, Mar. 4, 1913, inaugural ed.: 8. illus. Newsp

324

Chase, Salmon P. Letter, 1865 Mar. 4, Washington, D.C., to Mrs. Lincoln [Washington, D.C.] 1 p. Mss

Holograph signed, with envelope.

Transmits, as a "souvenir of a memorable day," "the Bible kissed by your honored husband, on taking today, for the second time the oath of office as President of the United States."

In the Robert Todd Lincoln Collection of the Papers of Abraham Lincoln, v. 191.

325

Coolidge to swear on Bible by which he learned to read. Evening star (Washington), Mar. 3, 1925: 2. Newsp

326

Eisenhower to use 2 Bibles. Washington post, Jan. 18, 1953: 15M. Newsp

327

Folliard, Edward T. President to take oath on mother's gift Bible. Washington post, Jan. 19, 1957: A-1, B-1. Newsp

328

Harding to kiss the Bible Washington's lips pressed. Evening star (Washington), Feb. 23, 1921: 3. Newsp

329

[Historic Bible] Illustrated London news, v. 158, Mar. 26, 1921: 415. AP4.I3, v. 158

Pictures of the Bible used at Washington's first inauguration and again by Harding in 1921.

330

Historic table again to hold inaugural Bible. Washington post, Jan. 19, 1941: B5. Newsp

331

The inaugural Bible; use of Holy Writ in swearing in the President. Washington post, Mar. 4, 1905, pt. 2: 1. Newsp

332
Looks over inaugural Bible; President elect to use old family holy book. Roosevelt selects passage from Bible for inaugural oath. Evening star (Washington), Feb. 28, 1933: 4. illus. Newsp

333
Moyer, William J. Bibles of the Presidents. Evening star (Washington), Jan. 20, 1953, special inaugural rotogravure section: 23. illus. Newsp

334
Moyer, William J. The George Washington Bible. Washington star pictorial magazine, Jan. 18, 1953: 1-2. illus. Newsp

Used by Eisenhower.

335
Nannes, Caspar. The Bible Kennedy chose for oath. Evening star (Washington), Jan. 20, 1961: AA-19. Newsp

336
President with Bibles he will use today. New York times, Jan. 20, 1949: 4. illus. Newsp

337
Prized as keepsake–Bible used in swearing in the President. Sunday star (Washington), Feb. 14, 1909, pt. 1: 5. Newsp

338
Ripley, Josephine. Inauguration day spotlights Bible. Christian science monitor, Dec. 15, 1960: 5. illus. Newsp

339
Robb, Inez. Matthew 5:3-11 ... Exodus 20:3-17. Times-herald (Washington), Jan. 20, 1949: 2. illus. Newsp

340
Roosevelt will take oath on old family Bible. *In* The Washington post. Inaugural edition, Saturday, March 4, 1933. Washington, 1933. p. 12. E806.W28

Illustration and caption only; no other text.

341
[Taft's inaugural Bible] Washington post, Mar. 4, 1909: 1. illus. Newsp

342
Third term Bible. Sunday star (Washington), Jan. 19, 1941, pt. 1: 5. illus. Newsp

343
Truman chooses the Beatitudes. Washington post, Jan. 20, 1949: 7. illus. Newsp

344
[Truman's inaugural Bible] Evening star (Washington), Jan. 17, 1949: B-1. illus. Newsp

A facsimile edition of the Gutenberg Bible.

345
Wright, John. Historic Bibles in America. New York, T. Whittaker [c1905] 222 p. facsims., plates (part col.) Z7771.A5W94

"Bibles Owned by the Presidents of the United States and Their Families": p. 27-57.

Bibles used at inaugurations are identified.

MUSIC

346
Apropos inaugurals. Musical America, v. 81, Mar. 1961: 29. group port. ML1.M384, v. 81

347
Bandsmen seek only perfection for THE parade. Washington post, Jan. 16, 1957: A12. illus. Newsp

348
Bernard, Kenneth A. Lincoln and the music of the Civil War. pt. 1. Hail to the Chief. Lincoln herald, v. 63, spring 1961: 29-35. illus. E457.M887, v. 63

References: p. 34-35.

About the music played at the inaugural ball on Mar. 4, 1861.

349
Bradley, Wendell P. Inauguration composer tells of his 'Declaration.' Washington post, Jan. 18, 1957: A3. port. Newsp

Morton Gould describes a new composition to receive its first performance at the inaugural concert on Jan. 20.

350
Concert program for inaugural day. Evening star (Washington), Feb. 18, 1925: 3. Newsp

351
Eisenhower keeps old promise; Ohio choir to sing at inaugural. New York herald-tribune, Jan. 10, 1953: 2. Newsp

352
Furman, Bess. Kennedy picks American music for inaugural concert, Jan. 19. New York times, Dec. 29, 1960: 12. Newsp

353
Hoffman, Jay K. From 1789 to 1961; inaugural music since Washington's day. New York times, Jan. 15, 1961, section 2: 9. Newsp

354
Hume, Paul. Pink elephants and roses: notables fill Constitution Hall for gala inaugural concert. Washington post, Jan. 19, 1953: 1. Newsp

355
Inaugural concerts; origin of prominent part of the exercises; both music and song. Marine Band always prominent feature. Evening star (Washington), Mar. 4, 1905, pt. 2: 2. Newsp

356
Kean, Charles D. Epiphany bells. Christian century, v. 78, Feb. 1, 1961: 158. BR1.C45, v. 78

"The [Church of the] Epiphany chimes have been used as part of the inaugural ceremony in all recent inductions of the President except that in 1957."

357

Lawrence, Harold. Inauguration concert. Audio, v. 49, Mar. 1965: 8.
TK6540.R17, v. 49

358

Musicales are planned for inaugural; 'Court of Freedom' erected in front of White House to be feature. Washington post, Dec. 6, 1940: 25.
Newsp

359

Poteete, Robert A. Inauguration poses puzzle to Marine Band: its 154-year-old archives fail to tell who rates ruffles and flourishes. New York herald-tribune, Dec. 23, 1952: 9. Newsp

360

Rosenfeld, Stephen S. Only classical music scheduled for inaugural. Washington post, Dec. 29, 1960: A-5. Newsp

361

Washington, D.C. Inaugural Committee, *1897.* Programs of the inaugural grand concerts, Pension Building, March 5 and 6, 1897, Washington, D.C. [Washington] Gibson Bros. Prs. [1897] 7 p. Rare Bk. Coll.

Copy also in DWP, in McKinley folder.

362

Washington, D.C. Inaugural Committee, *1901.* Programmes, inaugural grand concerts, Pension Building, Washington, D.C., March 5 and 6, nineteen hundred and one. [Washington, 1901] 7 p. DWP

In McKinley folder.

363

Washington, D.C. Inaugural Committee, *1909.* Inaugural grand concerts, Taft and Sherman, Pension Building, Washington, D.C., March 5th & 6th, 1909. [Washington] Crane Print. Co. [1909] [13] p. ports.
Rare Bk. Coll.

Copy also in DWP, in Taft folder.

364

Washington, D.C. Inaugural Committee, *1933.* Official inaugural concert ... Constitution Hall, Washington, D.C., Friday evening, March the third, nineteen hundred and thirty-three. [Washington? 1933?] [4] p. port. DWP

In F. D. Roosevelt 1933 folder.

WEATHER

365

Barbee, David R. Freaks of weather often spoil inaugural services; first five found skies clear, but with cold always on tap. *In* The Washington post. Inaugural edition, Saturday, March 4, 1933. Washington, 1933. p. 10. E806.W28

Table shows weather conditions on inauguration days from 1801 through 1929.

366

Collier, Rex. Next inauguration will be held in dead of winter; bugaboo of inaugural weather will be real cause of concern in the future, now that the date of ceremonies has been changed from March four to January twenty. Sunday star (Washington), Mar. 5, 1933, pt. 7: 10. illus. Newsp

367

Hayden, Mercedes P. Inauguration and the weather hazard. Washington post, Jan. 27, 1929, magazine: 1, 3. illus. Newsp

368

In fair weather ... and foul. Evening star (Washington), Jan. 21, 1957, inaugural souvenir section: 17. illus. Newsp

369

Inaugural day weather. Science news letter, v. 62, Dec. 27, 1952: 402. Q1.S76, v. 62

370

Inaugural weather through the years. Evening star (Washington), Jan. 20, 1953, special inaugural rotogravure section: 9. illus. Newsp

371

Inauguration day. Science, v. 77, Mar. 3, 1933: suppl., 8. Q1.S35, v. 77

372
Inauguration day weather forecast on past averages: even bet that Mr. Harding will need heavy overcoat, probably umbrella and overshoes. Evening star (Washington), Feb. 28, 1921: 17. Newsp

373
Often bad weather inauguration day; Washington reputation for inclemency is nation wide and century old. Sunday star (Washington), Mar. 4, 1917, pt. 1: 16. Newsp

374
Rauh, Donald M. The great day sometimes is a mean one. Evening star (Washington), Jan. 15, 1953: A-18. illus. Newsp

375
Thomson, Peggy. Inauguration day ... it has brought rain, snow, clouds and sun. Washington post Potomac, Jan. 17, 1965: 6-13. illus.
Newsp

376
Varied weather marks inaugurals; prior to Civil War, skies were friendly, but since reverse has been true. Evening star (Washington), Mar. 3, 1925: 11. Newsp

377
Weather at 1865 inaugural as seen by Walt Whitman. *In* The Washington post. Inaugural edition, Saturday, March 4, 1933. Washington, 1933. p. 2. E806.W28

378
Weather Bureau cautiously avoids inaugural prediction; forecast will be made when regular time comes, guarding 89 per cent batting average of 10 years. Evening star (Washington), Feb. 28, 1929: 4. Newsp

Includes brief notes on inaugural weather from 1861 through 1925.

379
Weather hit 3 inaugurals. Washington herald, Mar. 14, 1929: 22.
Newsp

Refers to the inaugurations of 1873, 1889, and 1909.

380
Worst inaugural day: March 4, 1873, holds the record for bad weather. Washington post, Mar. 4, 1905, pt. 2: 2. Newsp

CHANGE OF INAUGURATION DAY

381
About the new inaugural date. Mayflower's log, Jan. 1937: 20, 22-23. F191.W39, 1937

382
Archbald, Thomas F. The date of inauguration. Outlook, v. 91, Apr. 17, 1909: 868-869. AP2.O8, v. 91

383
Better inauguration date? Washington post, Jan. 21, 1961: A-12. Newsp

384
Both old and new inauguration days were selected by chance. Washington post, Jan. 20, 1937: 12-B. Newsp

385
[Changing the date of the inauguration] Nation, v. 88, Mar. 11, 1909: 237. AP2.N2, v. 88

386
Dangers of January inaugurations. Literary digest, v. 115, Apr. 22, 1933: 35. AP2.L58, v. 115

387
Dougherty, J. Hampden. Presidential succession problems, and change of inaugural day. Forum, v. 42, Dec. 1909: 523-533. AP2.F8, v. 42

388
Field, Kate. Change inauguration day. Kate Field's Washington, v. 7, Mar. 15, 1893: 162-163. AP2.K27, v. 7

389
Flynn, Michael W. Inauguration ceremonies in spring urged; President would simply take office in January, under method advanced by Krock. Washington herald, Jan. 22, 1937: 9. Newsp

390

The fourth of March. Nation, v. 42, Apr. 1, 1886: 274-275.
AP2.N2, v. 42

391

Frederic, Katherine A. Popular will postponed. Washington, Published by the Dept. of Efficiency in Government, National League of Women Voters, 1929. 11 p. JK550.F7

"A summary of the origin, history, and provisions of proposals relating to the 'Lame Duck' amendment."—p. 3.

392

Holland, Cecil. President urges earlier elections and inaugurals. Evening star (Washington), Jan. 18, 1961: A-1, A-6. Newsp

393

The inauguration and the weather. Outlook, v. 91, Mar. 13, 1909: 566-567. AP2.O8, v. 91

Urges inauguration date be changed.

394

Inauguration day. Outlook, v. 81, Dec. 9, 1905: 855-856.
AP2.O8, v. 81

Plea for change in date.

395

Larson, Cedric. Watch induction in winter; citizens of United States have given years of attention to merits of various dates, and now hope that new January ceremony will prove successful. Sunday star (Washington), Jan. 17, 1937, pt. 4: 2, 7. Newsp

396

Lincoln, Gould. Inauguration rites in spring urged. Evening star (Washington), Mar. 9, 1957: A-4. Newsp

Advocates indoor ceremony or postponement of outdoor inaugural until late spring to avoid risk to President's health. *See also* letter on this subject, from George F. Miller, published on the same page.

397

Mussman, Michael A. Changing date of inauguration day. American political science review, v. 18, Feb. 1924: 113-118. JA1.A6, v. 18

387

Not April 30 but December 1. Outlook, v. 94, Feb. 26, 1910: 424-425. AP2.O8, v. 94

399

O'Leary, J. A. Early inaugural plan again waits on House. Sunday star (Washington), June 16, 1929, pt. 2: 3. Newsp

400

On dead center. Outlook, v. 127, Jan. 5, 1921: 12. AP2.O8, v. 127

401

Polk, James K., *Pres. U.S.* Speech of Mr. Polk, on the proposition to amend the Constitution of the United States, respecting the election of President and Vice President. Delivered in the House of Representatives, March 13, 1826. [Washington, 1826] 32 p. (Miscellaneous pamphlets, v. 250, no. 17) AC901.M5, v. 250 Rare Bk. Coll.

402

Should inauguration day and sessions of Congress be changed? Congressional digest, v. 5, Aug./Sept. 1926: 219-240. JK1.C65, v. 5

403

U.S. *70th Congress, 1st session, 1927-1928. House.* Fixing the Presidential and Congressional term. Proceedings and debate in the House of Representatives on S.J. Res. 47 proposing an amendment to the Constitution of the United States fixing the commencement of the terms of President and Vice President and Members of Congress and fixing the time of the assembling of Congress. Washington, U.S. Govt. Print. Off., 1928. 87 p. ([U.S.] 70th Congress, 1st session. House document 331) JK538.1928.A3

404

U.S. *Congress. House.* Terms of President, Vice President, Senators and Representatives. Compiled and issued by the House Document Room, House of Representatives. Carl G. Malmberg, superintendent. Washington, Govt. Print. Off., 1922. 36 p. JK550.A5 1922

405

U.S. *Congress. House. Committee on Election of President, Vice President, and Representatives in Congress.* Change of date of inauguration. ... December 16, 1909. ... Statement of Hon. Henry B. F. Macfarland. [Washington, Govt. Print. Off., 1910] 19 p. JK538.1910.A3

406

U.S. *Congress. House. Committee on Election of President, Vice President, and Representatives in Congress.* Memorandum upon proposed constitutional amendment changing terms of President, Vice President, Senators, and Representatives. Washington, Govt. Print. Off., 1924. 19 p. JK550.A5 1924a

Confidential committee print on H.J. Res. 93.

407

U.S. *Congress. House. Committee on Election of President, Vice President, and Representatives in Congress.* Proposed amendment to the Constitution of the United States fixing the commencement of the terms of President and Vice President and Members of Congress, and fixing the time of the assembling of Congress. Hearings ..., Sixty-eighth Congress, first session. H.J. Res. 93. January 10 and January 24 [March 27] 1924. Washington, Govt. Print. Off., 1924. 2 pts. JK538.1924.A3

408

U.S. *Congress. House. Committee on Election of President, Vice President, and Representatives in Congress.* Proposed amendment to the Constitution of the United States fixing the commencement of the terms of President and Vice President and Members of Congress, and fixing the time of the assembling of Congress. Hearings ..., Sixty-ninth Congress, first session on H.J. Res. 56, H.J. Res. 164, S.J. Res. 9 proposing an amendment to the Constitution of the United States. January 18 and February 22, 1926. Washington, Govt. Print. Off., 1926. 26 p. JK170 1926

409

U.S. *Congress. House. Committee on Election of President, Vice President, and Representatives in Congress.* Proposed constitutional amendments relating to the fixing of the time for the commencement of the terms of President, Vice President, and Members of Congress, and fixing the time of the assembling of Congress, etc. Hearings ..., Seventieth Congress,

325-882 O-69—5

first session. H.J. Res. 65, H. Con. Res. 4, H.J. Res. 30, H.J. Res. 95. Monday, December 19, 1927. Washington, U.S. Govt. Print. Off., 1928. 8 p. JK170 1927d

410

U.S. *Congress. House. Committee on Election of President, Vice President, and Representatives in Congress.* Proposed constitutional amendments relating to the fixing of the time for the commencement of the terms of President, Vice President, and Members of Congress, and fixing the time of the assembling of Congress; and to the Presidential succession; and to the Electoral College system. Hearings ..., Seventy-first Congress, second session. H.J. Res. 65, H.J. Res. 9, H.J. Res. 216, H.J. Res. 292. February 4, 7, 14, and 21, 1930. Washington, U.S. Govt. Print. Off., 1930. 67 p. JK550.A5 1930

411

U.S. *Congress. House. Committee on the Judiciary.* Hearing ... in relation to H.J. Res. 55 and H.J. Res. 90 [59th Congress, 1st session, concerning the proposed change of inauguration day] Washington, Govt. Print. Off., 1906. 70 p. JK540.A3 1906

Letter from H. B. F. Macfarland, chairman of the National Committee on the Proposed Change of Inauguration Day, dated Jan. 18, 1906, enclosing extracts from letters written by governors of States and Territories and others, together with editorials from various newspapers.

412

U.S. *Congress. House. Committee on the Judiciary.* Inauguration day. [Washington, 1903] 12 p. JK540.A3 1903

413

U.S. *Congress. House. Committee on the Judiciary.* Term of office of President, Vice-President, etc. Report to accompany H.J. Res. 115. [Washington, Govt. Print. Off., 1910] 6 p. ([U.S.] 61st Congress, 2d session. House report 121) JK550.A5 1910

414

U.S. *Congress. House. Committee on the Judiciary.* Terms of President, Vice President, Senators, and Representatives. Report to accompany H.J. Res. 204. [Washington, Govt. Print. Off., 1912] 25 p. ([U.S.] 62d Congress, 2d session. House report 239) JK550.A5 1912

415
U.S. *Congress. Senate. Committee on the Judiciary.* Change of inauguration date. Report ... by the subcommittee appointed to consider and report on Senate Joint Resolution 27 proposing an amendment to the Constitution of the United States. Washington, Govt. Print. Off., 1912. 5 p. JK540.A3 1912

416
U.S. *Congress. Senate. Committee on the Judiciary.* Fixing the commencement of terms of President, Vice President, and Members of Congress. Report to accompany S.J. Res. 22. [Washington, Govt. Print. Off., 1924] 5 p. ([U.S.] 68th Congress, 1st session. Senate report 170) JK550.A5 1924

417
U.S. *Congress. Senate. Committee on the Judiciary.* Fixing the commencement of the terms of the President and Vice President and Members of Congress. Report to accompany S.J. Res. 47. [Washington, U.S. Govt. Print. Off., 1927] 5 p. ([U.S.] 70th Congress, 1st session. Senate report 5) JK550.A5 1927

418
U.S. *Congress. Senate. Committee on the Judiciary.* Proposed change in terms of President, Vice President, and Members of Congress. Hearing ..., 67th Congress, 4th session, on S.J. Res. 8, proposing an amendment to the Constitution of the United States. Also S.J. Res. 53, 54, 86 and 151, 67th Cong. December 5, 1922. Washington, Govt. Print. Off., 1923. 14 p. JK550.A5 1922b

419
Wright, Herbert F. The change of inauguration date. Catholic world, v. 112, Mar. 1921: 815-822. AP2.C3, v. 112

INDIVIDUAL INAUGURATIONS
George Washington

420
Adams, John Quincy, *Pres. U.S.* The jubilee of the Constitution. A discourse delivered at the request of the New York Historical Society, in the city of New York, on Tuesday, the 30th of April, 1839; being the fiftieth anniversary of the inauguration of George Washington as

President of the United States, on Thursday, the 30th of April, 1789. New York, S. Colman, 1839. 136 p. front. JK119.A4

"An account of the celebration by the New York Historical Society of the 50th anniversary of Washington's inauguration": p. [121]-136.

421

Alden, John. Souvenir and official programme of the centennial celebration of George Washington's inauguration as first President of the United States. New York, Garnett & Gow, c1889. 393 p. illus.

E312.6.A35

422

Andrews, William L. New York as Washington knew it after the Revolution. New York, C. Scribner's Sons, 1905. 91 p. illus.

F128.44.A56 Rare Bk. Coll.

Ceremonies and festivities at Washington's first inauguration: p. 39-50.

423

Bacheller, Irving, *and* Herbert S. Kates. Great moments in the life of Washington. [New York] Grosset & Dunlap [c1932] 159 p. illus.

E312.B18

First inauguration: p. 133.
Second inauguration: p. 145.

424

Bancroft, Aaron. Life of George Washington, Commander in Chief of the American Army through the Revolutionary War, and the first President of the United States. London, Printed for J. Stockdale, 1808. 560 p.

E312.B22

First inauguration and address: p. 372-378.

425

Bankers Trust Company, *New York.* Wall & Nassau; an account of the inauguration of George Washington in Federal Hall at Wall and Nassau Streets, April 30, 1789. New York, Bankers Trust Co. [c1939] 81 p. illus. (part col.) E311.B35

426

Barbee, David R. First inauguration impressive event; Washington's journey to New York City triumphant demonstration. *In* The

Washington post. Inaugural edition, Saturday, March 4, 1933. Washington, 1933. p. 2. E806.W28

427

Barbee, David R. Religious service ended procession; Washington and escort went to St. Paul's for rites. *In* The Washington post. Inaugural edition, Saturday, March 4, 1933. Washington, 1933. p. 12.
E806.W28

428

Bloom, Sol. The inauguration of George Washington. American foreign service journal, v. 16, Apr. 1939: 198-199, 225-227. illus.
JX1.A53, v. 16

429

Bowen, Clarence W. The centennial celebration of the inauguration of George Washington as first President of the United States, Monday, Tuesday and Wednesday, April 29th, 30th, and May 1st, 1889. Official programme with historical sketches. [New York?] c1889. 36 p.
E312.6.B78

430

Bowen, Clarence W., *ed.* The history of the centennial celebration of the inauguration of George Washington as first President of the United States. New York, D. Appleton, 1892. xviii, 673 p. illus.
E312.6.B785

431

Bowen, Clarence W. The inauguration of Washington. Century magazine, v. 37, Apr. 1889: 803-833. illus. AP2.C4, v. 37

432

Brown, Everett S. The inauguration of George Washington. Michigan alumnus quarterly review, v. 45, spring 1939: 213-221. illus.
AP2.M53, v. 45

Reprinted in his *The Territorial Delegate to Congress and Other Essays* (Ann Arbor, Mich., George Wahr Pub. Co., 1950. JK21.B7), p. 54-68.

433

Calver, William L. Washington inaugural buttons. *In* New York Historical Society. Quarterly bulletin, v. 9, Jan. 1926: 124-126. illus.
F116.N638, v. 9

434

Campbell, Amelia D. The last Washington inaugural flag. Daughters of the American Revolution magazine, v. 55, Oct. 1921: 581-583. illus.
E202.5.A12, v. 55

435

Cloud, Archibald J., *and* Vierling Kersey. Episodes in the life of George Washington. New York, C. Scribner's Sons [c1932] 226 p. illus.
E312.C64

First inauguration: p. 143-149.
Second inauguration: p. 155-156.
Inauguration of John Adams: p. 157.

436

Coffin, Charles C. The first Presidential inauguration. Chautauquan, v. 9, Apr. 1889: 401-403. AP2.C48, v. 9

437

Curtis, George W. An address at the unveiling of the statue of Washington, upon the spot where he took the oath as first President of the United States. Delivered on the (25th) 26th November, 1883, the one hundredth anniversary of the evacuation of the city of New York by the British Army. New York, Harper, 1883. 35 p. front.
F128.64.W31C9

438

De La Bedoyere, Michael. George Washington. Philadelphia, J. B. Lippincott Co. [1935] 309 p. E312.D46

First inauguration: p. 247-248.
Inauguration of John Adams: p. 284.

439

Dowe, Charles E. The inauguration of the first President. Cosmopolitan, v. 6, Apr. 1889: 533-543. illus. AP2.C8, v. 6

440
First inaugural: only five hundred men marched in the parade. Evening star (Washington), Jan. 26, 1901: 9. Newsp

441
First inaugural, used as a model now, was impromptu ceremony. Evening star (Washington), Mar. 3, 1925: 11. Newsp

442
Flynn, John T. The first inauguration. Reader's digest, v. 54, Feb. 1949: 91-93. illus. AP2.R255, v. 54

443
Freeman, Douglas Southhall. George Washington, a biography. New York, Scribner, 1948- [57] 7 v. illus. E312.F82

First inauguration: v. 6, p. 185-198.
Second inauguration: v. 7, p. 7-9.
Inauguration of John Adams: v. 7, p. 436-437.

444
Fuller, Melville W. Address in commemoration of the inauguration of George Washington as first President of the United States, delivered before the two Houses of Congress, December 11, 1889. Washington, Govt. Print. Off., 1890. 39 p. E312.63.F962

445
Griswold, Rufus W. The republican court; or, American society in the days of Washington. A new ed., with the author's last additions and corrections. New York, D. Appleton, 1864. 481 p. ports. E164.G87

Washington's first inauguration: p. [137]-146.

446
Guiterman, Arthur. The first inauguration. Saturday evening post, v. 201, Mar. 2, 1929: 60. AP2.S2, v. 201

Poem.

447
Hall, Charles C. A sermon to commemorate the inauguration of President Washington on 30 April, A.D. 1789. Preached in the First Presbyterian

Church, Brooklyn, N.Y., on 28 April, A.D. 1889. New York, Press of L. Belcher [1889] 22 p. E312.63.H15

448

Hart, Albert B. Washington as President. Washington, George Washington Bicentennial Commission, 1931. 41 p. illus. (Honor to George Washington. Pamphlet no. 8) E312.H77, no. 8

Reprinted in the *History of the George Washington Bicentennial Celebration,* Literature Series, v. 1 (Washington, 1932. E312.6.U58, v. 1), p. 83-94.

First inauguration: p. 3-4 (reprint, p. 84).

449

The inaugural of our first President and historic notes relating to the life and times of George Washington. N[ew] Y[ork], Moss Engraving Co., 1889. [16] p. illus. E312.6.I35

450

Irving, Washington. Life of George Washington. New York, G. P. Putnam, 1855-59. 5 v. illus. E312.I6

First inauguration: v. 4, p. 512-515.
Second inauguration: v. 5, p. 144-145.
Inauguration of John Adams: v. 5, p. 270-271.

451

Johnston, Elizabeth B., *comp.* George Washington day by day. New York, Cycle Pub. Co., 1895. xv, 207 p. E312.15.J732

First inauguration: p. 64.
Second inauguration: p. 35.
Inauguration of John Adams: p. 35.

452

Kennedy, Will P. First inaugural address found; Senate Library held historical document. Evening star (Washington), Apr. 26, 1933: B-1. illus. Newsp

See item 481.

453

[The Lacour-Doolittle Federal Hall] *In* Stokes, I. N. Phelps. The iconography of Manhattan Island, 1498-1909. v. 3. New York, R. H. Dodd, 1918. p. [537]-539. illus. F128.37.S87, v. 3

Describes Mr. Stokes' copy of "the only known contemporary representation of Washington's inauguration." The engraving is reproduced as frontispiece I in the same volume.

454

Lamb, Martha J. R. (Nash). The inauguration of Washington, 1789. Magazine of American history, v. 20, Dec. 1888: 433-460. illus.

E171.M18, v. 20

Reprinted, with two other papers, in her *Souvenir of the Centennial Anniversary of Washington's Inauguration* (New York, White and Allen, c1889. 86 p. E312.6.L2).

455

Lamb, Martha J. R. (Nash). The story of the Washington centennial. Magazine of American history, v. 22, July 1889: 1-36. illus.

E171.M18, v. 22

456

Lombard, M. E. The inauguration of George Washington. Légion d'honneur magazine, v. 9, Apr. 1939: 293-300. port.

CR5061.U6A3, v. 9

457

Lorant, Stefan. Milestones of the Republic: other inaugurations recalled; Washington's, April 30, 1789. Times-herald (Washington), Jan. 16, 1949: 1, 4. illus. Newsp

458

Lossing, Benson J. Description of First in Peace. (With key plate.) Representing the arrival of Gen'l Geo. Washington at the Battery, New York, April 23, 1789, previous to his inauguration as the first President of the United States, April 30, 1789. Painted by A. Rivey, Paris, from a cartoon by H. Brueckner. Engraved on steel by John C. McRae. London, New York, J. Laing [1889] 8 p. illus. E312.43.L88

459

Lossing, Benson J. Life of Washington; a biography, personal, military, and political. New York, Virtue [1860] 3 v. illus. E312.L88

First inauguration: v. 3, p. 92-96.
Second inauguration: v. 3, p. 233-234.
Inauguration of John Adams: v. 3, p. 472-475.

460

McMaster, John B. Washington's inauguration. Harper's monthly magazine, v. 78, Apr. 1889: 671-686. illus. AP2.H3, v. 78

461

Matteson, David M. George Washington every day; a calendar of events and principles of his entire lifetime. [Washington, United States George Washington Bicentennial Commission, 1933] p. 321-576. illus. E312.15.M27

First inauguration: p. 394.
Second inauguration: p. 359.
Inauguration of John Adams: p. 360.
Originally published as part of the *History of the George Washington Bicentennial Celebration,* Literature Series, v. 3 (Washington, 1932. E312.6.U58, v. 3), p. 321-565.

462

Monaghan, Frank. Notes on the inaugural journey and the inaugural ceremonies of George Washington as first President of the United States. [New York] Prepared for private distribution, 1939. 52 (*i.e.* 48) l. E311.M6

"Pages 19 to 22 have been deleted."—Leaf 18.

----- -----Supplementary notes on the inaugural journey and the inaugural ceremonies of George Washington as first President of the United States. [New York] Prepared for private distribution, 1939. 51 l. E311.M6 Suppl.

463

Monahon, Clifford P. Richard Bache's letter to his wife describing the inauguration of Washington, as depicted in the John Brown House scenic wall paper. Rhode Island history, v. 7, Apr. 1948: 57-59. illus. F76.R472, v. 7

Reproduces text of letter; illustration shows scenic wallpaper in dining room of John Brown House.

464

Nation honors Washington; inaugural re-enacted here. New York times, Feb. 23, 1949: 1, 14. Newsp

465

New York (City) Committee on Centennial Celebration of the Inauguration of Washington. Centennial celebration of the inauguration of

George Washington as President of the United States. 1789-1889. [Boston, Printed by the Boston Photogravure Co., 1889] 12 p. illus.
E312.6.N564

466

New York tribune. The Washington centenary celebrated in New-York April 29, 30–May 1, 1889. New-York, Tribune Association [1889] 120 p. illus. (Library of Tribune extras. v. 1. May 1889. no. 5)
E312.6.N53

467

Newman, Oliver P. First American inaugural parade from Mount Vernon to New York. Sunday star (Washington), Mar. 1, 1925, pt. 5: 2, 6. illus.
Newsp

468

Peter's journal of the first presidential count and Washington's inauguration, showing how Vice-President Adams got ahead in the ceremony. Edited by "Historicus." New York, Printed for the Proprietor, 1885. 24 p.
E311.P47

469

Presidential inaugurations: Washington–1789. Ladies' magazine and literary gazette, v. 4, Oct. 1831: 435-440.
AP2.A343, v. 4

"... by a distinguished lady of Washington."

470

Quincy, Eliza S. (Morton). Memoir of the life of Eliza S. M. Quincy. Boston [Printed by J. Wilson] 1861. 267 p.
E302.6.Q7Q74

Washington's first inauguration: p. 51-52.

471

Saunders, Frederick, *comp.* The Washington centennial souvenir. New York, T. Whittaker, 1889. 41 p. illus.
E312.6.S25

Contents. Sketch of the inauguration of Washington. Tributes of genius and affection to the memory of Washington. Memorabilia.

472

1789-1889; the Washington inauguration centenary. Historic scenes, and three days' commemorative celebrations. Frank Leslie's illustrated newspaper, v. 68, May 4, 1889: 202-203. illus.
AP2.L52, v. 68

Illustrations on p. 197, 204, 205; four-page foldout on p. 214-215/218-219.

473

Smith, Thomas E. V. The city of New York in the year of Washington's inauguration, 1789. New York, A. D. F. Randolph, 1889. 244 p. fold. map. F128.44.S67

Washington's first inauguration: p. 228-235.

474

Smucker, Isaac. A great event of a century ago: Washington's inauguration and inaugural. Magazine of western history, v. 9, Mar. 1889: 522-526. E171.N27, v. 9

475

Souvenir of the centennial celebration of Washington's inauguration, held in New York City, April 29th and 30th, 1889. New York, Nicoll & Roy [c1889] 112 p. illus. E312.6.S72

Contents., The inauguration of George Washington, by C. E. Dowe. Official programme. A convenient and trustworthy guide to New York City.

476

Sparks, Jared. The life of George Washington. Boston, F. Andrews, 1839. xix, 562 p. illus. E312.S73

First inauguration: p. 408-410.
Second inauguration: p. 445.
Inauguration of John Adams: p. 476.

477

Stone, William L. Setting the wheels in motion. *In his* Tales and sketches,–such as they are. v. 2. New-York, Harper, 1834. p. [171]-216. PS2943.S85T3, v. 2 Rare Bk. Coll.

Inauguration of Washington: p. 194-203.
First inaugural ball: p. 204-209.

478

Tebbel, John W. George Washington's America. New York, Dutton, 1954. 478 p. map. E312.27.T4

First inauguration: p. 261-267.

479

Towner, Ausburn. Our first President's inauguration. Frank Leslie's popular monthly, v. 27, Apr. 1889: 385-396. illus. AP2.A346, v. 27

480

U.S. *Constitution Sesquicentennial Commission.* George Washington, the President; triumphant journey as President-elect; first term of the first President. 1789-1939. Washington [U.S. Govt. Print. Off., 1939] 32 p. illus. E311.U56

481

U.S. *President, 1789-1797 (Washington)* Washington's inaugural address of 1789. [Washington, U.S. Govt. Print. Off., 1952] 14 p. facsim. ([U.S.] National Archives. Facsimile no. 22) E173.U6, no. 22

Reproduction of a holograph of the address delivered Apr. 30, 1789, from the records of the Senate, with explanatory text.

482

U.S. *President, 1789-1797 (Washington)* Washington's inaugurals. [Boston, Directors of the Old South Work, 1896] 12 p. (Old South leaflets. [General series, v. 1] no. 10) E173.O44, v. 1

Contains also "The Inauguration of Washington" from Irving's *Life of Washington.*

483

Washburn, Mabel T. R. Election and inauguration of Washington as President and the beginning of the United States Government under the Constitution; a contemporaneous account ... gathered out of newspapers of that day. Journal of American history, v. 8, Apr./June 1914: 181-220. illus. E171.J86, v. 8

484

The Washington centennial. Critic, v. 14, May 4, 1889: 225-227. AP2.C92, v. 14

485

The Washington centennial. 1789-1889. [New York, Press of Farrand and Everdell, c1889] 32, 7 p. illus. E312.6.W28

486

The Washington Centennial Loan Exhibition. Critic, v. 14, Apr. 20, 1889: 199. AP2.C93, v. 14

487

The "Washington flag."*In* New York *(City) Art Commission.* Annual report. 1921. [New York, 1922?] p. 11-16. illus.

N6535.N5A3, 1921

Describes a flag used at Washington's first inauguration, now deposited in the Metropolitan Museum of Art for exhibition and safekeeping.

488

Washington's inauguration as first President of the United States, New York City, April 30th, 1789. Frank Leslie's illustrated newspaper, v. 68, May 4, 1889: 217. AP2.L52, v. 68

489

Whitney, Frank C. Inaugural ceremonies of President Washington. *In* Groton, Mass. Citizens. Centennial anniversary of Washington's inauguration. Proceedings in the First Parish Meeting-House, at Groton, Massachusetts, April 30, 1889. Groton, Printed for private distribution, 1889. p. 14-16. E312.6.G88

George Washington Second Inauguration

490

Thornton, Edward. [Letter to Sir James Bland Burges, Bart., dated Philadelphia, March 5, 1793] Pennsylvania magazine of history and biography, v. 9, July 1885: 219-220. F146.P65, v. 9

John Adams

491

Adams, Charles Francis. The life of John Adams. Begun by John Quincy Adams. Rev. and corr. Philadelphia, J. B. Lippincott, 1871. 2 v.

E322.A52

Inauguration: v. 2, p. 218-223.

492

Allison, John M. Adams and Jefferson, the story of a friendship. Norman, University of Oklahoma Press [1966] 349 p. E322.A6

Inauguration of John Adams: p. 153-154.
Jefferson's first inauguration: p. 227-228.

493

Barbee, David R. Washington stole show from Adams; people more interested in retiring President; inaugural simple. *In* The Washington post. Inaugural edition, Saturday, March 4, 1933. Washington, 1933. p. 12. E806.W28

494

Chinard, Gilbert. Honest John Adams. Boston, Little, Brown, 1933. 359 p. plates, ports. E322.C47

Inauguration: p. 259.

495

Gibbs, George. Memoirs of the administrations of Washington and John Adams, edited from the papers of Oliver Wolcott, Secretary of the Treasury. New York, Printed for the subscribers [W. Van Norden, printer] 1846. 2 v. port. E311.G44

Inauguration of John Adams: v. 1, p. 451-452.

496

Kurtz, Stephen G. The Presidency of John Adams; the collapse of Federalism, 1795-1800. Philadelphia, University of Pennsylvania Press [1957] 488 p. illus. E321.K8

Inauguration: p. 208, 222-224.

497

Morse, John T. John Adams. Boston, Houghton Mifflin, 1898. xxii, 338 p. (American statesmen, v. 6) E322.M882

Inauguration: p. 261-262.

498

[Presidential inaugurations:] Adams–1797. Ladies' magazine and literary gazette, v. 4, Oct. 1831: 440-441. AP2.A343, v. 4

499

Sedgwick, Theodore. [Letter, 12th March, 1797, Stockbridge, to Rufus King, London, on the Presidential election and inauguration] *In* King, Rufus. The life and correspondence. Edited by his grandson, Charles R. King. v. 2. 1795-1799. New York, G. P. Putnam's Sons, 1895. p. 156-159. E302.K54, v. 2

500

Smith, Page. John Adams. v. 2. 1784-1826. Garden City, N.Y., Doubleday, 1962. p. 602- 1170. plates, ports. E322.S64

Washington's first inauguration: p. 746-750.
Inauguration of John Adams: p. 917-920.

501

U.S. *President, 1797-1801 (John Adams)* John Adams. Inaugural address. [n.p., Americanization Dept., Veterans of Foreign Wars of the United States, 1926] 7 p. E321.U625

502

U.S. *President, 1797-1801 (John Adams)* John Adams's inaugural. Inaugural address at Philadelphia, March 4, 1797. [Boston, Directors of the Old South Work, 1902] 16 p. (Old South leaflets. [General series, v. 5] no. 103) E173.O44, v. 5

Thomas Jefferson

503

Barbee, David R. Jefferson first President inaugurated in Washington, new Capital of Nation. *In* The Washington post. Inaugural edition, Saturday, March 4, 1933. Washington, 1933. p. 6. E806.W28

504

Bowers, Claude G. Jefferson and Hamilton; the struggle for democracy in America. Boston, Houghton Mifflin Co., 1925. xvii, 531 p. facsims., plates, ports. E311.B65

Jefferson's first inauguration: p. 508-510.

505

Boykin, Edward. Jefferson swapped boardinghouse for mansion; simplicity marked his inauguration 150 years ago. Sunday star (Washington), Mar. 4, 1951: C-2. illus. Newsp

506

Busey, Samuel C. The centennial of the first inauguration of a President at the permanent seat of the Government. *In* Columbia Historical Society, *Washington, D.C.* Records. v. 5; 1901. Washington, 1902. p. 96-111. F191.C72, v. 5

507

Curtis, William E. The true Thomas Jefferson. Philadelphia, J. B. Lippincott Co., 1901. 395 p. facsims., plates, ports. (The "True" biographies) E332.C97

First inauguration: p. 186-189.

508

Davis, John. Travels of four years and a half in the United States of America; during 1798, 1799, 1800, 1801, and 1802. London, Sold by T. Ostell [etc.] and H. Caritat; New-York, for R. Edwards, printer, Bristol, 1803. 454 p. E164.D26

Jefferson's first inauguration and inaugural address: p. 177-185.

509

Hirst, Francis W. Life and letters of Thomas Jefferson. New York, Macmillan Co., 1926. xviii, 588 p. facsims., map, plates, ports. E332.H65

First inauguration: p. 378-379.
Second inauguration: p. 405-406.

510

Jefferson, Thomas, *Pres. U.S.* Jefferson himself, the personal narrative of a many-sided American, edited by Bernard Mayo. Boston, Houghton Mifflin Co., 1932. xv, 384 p. facsims., plans, plates, ports. E332.J464

First inauguration: p. 219-224.

511

Jefferson, Thomas. *Pres. U.S.* The speech of Thomas Jefferson, Esq., the newly elected President of the United States of America; to the Senate, House of Representatives, public officers, &c., on the 4th of March, 1801. With a few remarks on its probable effects. By an Englishman. London, Printed for Thurgood by W. S. Betham, 1801. 16 p. J82.A31 Mar. 4b Rare Bk. Coll.

512

Lorant, Stefan. Historian speaks: ceremony for Mr. Jefferson was first held in Washington. Times-herald (Washington), Jan. 17, 1949: 1, 7. Newsp

325-882 O-69—6

513

Padover, Saul K. Jefferson. New York, Harcourt, Brace [1942] 459 p. plates, ports. E332.P12

First inauguration: p. 290-294.
Second inauguration: p. 344-345.

514

Parton, James. Life of Thomas Jefferson, third President of the United States. Boston, Houghton Mifflin [1902] 764 p. port. E332.P28

First inauguration: p. 586-588.

515

Presidential inaugurations: Jefferson–1801. Ladies' magazine and literary gazette, v. 4, Nov. 1831: 481-485. AP2.A343, v. 4

516

Proctor, John C. In Jefferson's time, when the citizens of Washington voted and celebrated its first inauguration. Sunday star (Washington), Apr. 1, 1951: C-2. Newsp

517

Randall, Henry S. The life of Thomas Jefferson. New York, Derby & Jackson, 1858. 3 v. facsims., ports. E332.R18

First inauguration: v. 2, p. 630–634.
Second inauguration: v. 3, p. 132-134.

518

Ryan, Francis de Sales. Jefferson walked to Capitol: today is 150th anniversary of first inauguration here. Washington post, Mar. 4, 1951: 1, 9. Newsp

519

Schachner, Nathan. Thomas Jefferson, a biography. New York, Appleton-Century-Crofts [1951] 2 v. (1070 p.) illus., ports. E332.S32

First inauguration: p. 659-664.
Second inauguration: p. 795-796.

520

Shippen, Rebecca L. Inauguration of President Thomas Jefferson, 1801. Pennsylvania magazine of history and biography, v. 25, Apr. 1901: 71-76. F146.P65, v. 25

First published in the *Ladies' Magazine.*

521

Smith, W. H. Tradition vs. facts about the first inauguration in Washington. Washington post, Jan. 5, 1913, magazine section: 1. illus.
Newsp

522

U.S. *Library of Congress.* The Thomas Jefferson bicentennial, 1743-1943. A catalogue of the exhibitions at the Library of Congress opened on April 12th. Washington, U.S. Govt. Print. Off., 1943. 170 p. illus.
E332.U58

"Jefferson's First Inaugural Address": p. 23.

523

U.S. *President, 1801-1809 (Jefferson)* The address of Thomas Jefferson, to the Senate, the members of the House of Representatives, the public officers, and a large concourse of citizens. Delivered in the Senate chamber, on the 4th day of March, 1801, on his taking the oath of office, as President of the United States of America. Baltimore, Printed for Keatinge's Book-store, 1801. 8 p. E331.U56 Rare Bk. Coll.

524

U.S. *President, 1801-1809 (Jefferson)* Discorso del Signor Tommaso Jefferson, pronunziato il 4. marzo 1801. nella camera del Senato, in presenza del medesimo, dei membri della Camera dei rappresentanti, dei principali impiegati, e di un numeroso concorso di concittadini, prima di assumere la carica di presidente degli Stati Uniti Americani. [n.p., 1801] 8 p. (Political pamphlets, v. 101, no. 11)
JA36.P8, v. 101 Rare Bk. Coll.

Translated by Filippo Mazzei.

525

U.S. *President, 1801-1809 (Jefferson)* The inaugural address of Thomas Jefferson delivered March 4, 1801. Worcester, A. J. St. Onge, 1943. 31 p. 8 cm.
J82.A31 Mar. 4 Min. Case

"Published to commemorate the 200th anniversary of the birth of Thomas Jefferson."– p. [4].

526

U.S. *President, 1801-1809 (Jefferson)* The inaugural speeches and messages of Thomas Jefferson ... together with the inaugural speech of James Madison. Boston, Printed by S. G. Snelling, 1809. 126 p.

J82.A3 1809

527

U.S. *President, 1801-1809 (Jefferson)* Jefferson's inaugurals. First inaugural address at Washington, March 4, 1801. [Second inaugural address, March 4, 1805. Boston, Directors of the Old South Work, 1902] 16 p. (Old South leaflets. [General series, v. 5] no. 104)

E173.O44, v. 5

"Jefferson and His Inauguration. From Henry Adams's *History of the United States*": p. 10-15.

"Letter from Jefferson to Samuel Adams. Washington, Mar. 29, 1801": p. 15-16.

528

U.S. *President, 1801-1809 (Jefferson)* Speech of Thomas Jefferson, President of the United States, delivered at his instalment, March 4, 1801, at the city of Washington. [Washington? 1801] 16 p.

E331.U566 Rare Bk. Coll.

529

U.S. *President, 1801-1809 (Jefferson)* Speech of Thomas Jefferson, President of the United States, delivered at his instalment, March 4, 1801, at the city of Washington. To which are prefixed, his farewell address to the Senate: and a brief account of the proceedings at the instalment. Philadelphia, Printed by Cochran & M'Laughlin, for Mathew Carey, 1801. 24 p. (Political pamphlets, v. 101, no. 8)

JA36.P8, v. 101 Rare Bk. Coll.

Brief account of the proceedings: p. 8-10.

530

U.S. *President, 1801-1809 (Jefferson)* Speech of Thomas Jefferson, President of the United States, delivered at his instalment, March 4, 1801, at the city of Washington. With translations into the French, Italian, and German tongues. Paris, Printed at the English Press [1801] 16 p. (Political pamphlets, v. 101, no. 9)

JA36.P8, v. 101 Rare Bk. Coll.

531

U.S. *President, 1801-1809 (Jefferson)* Speech of Thomas Jefferson, President of the United States; delivered in the Senate chamber of the Capitol, the 4th of March at 12 o'clock. New-York, Printed by W. Durell, 1801. [13] p. front. E331.U567 Rare Bk. Coll.

Thomas Jefferson
Second Inauguration

532

U.S. *President, 1801-1809 (Jefferson)* President's speech. [Washington, 1805] 8 p. (Duane pamphlets, v. 93, no. 8) AC901.D8, v. 93

Second inaugural address.

James Madison

533

Anthony, Katharine S. Dolly Madison, her life and times. Garden City, N.Y., Doubleday, 1949. 426 p. E342.1.A58

First inauguration: p. 191-194.

534

Brant, Irving. James Madison. v. 5. The President, 1809-1812. Indianapolis, Bobbs-Merrill [1956] 540 p. facsims., plates, ports. E342.B7, v. 5

First inauguration: p. 11-21.

535

Clark, Allen C. Life and letters of Dolly Madison. Washington, Press of W. F. Roberts Co., 1914. 517 p. plates, ports. E342.1.C5

Washington's inaugural balls: p. 97-98.
Madison's first inauguration and ball: p. 99-102.
Madison's second inauguration and ball: p. 148-149.

536

Eaton, Dorothy S. Acquisition notes. *In* U.S. *Library of Congress.* Information bulletin, v. 17, May 12, 1958: 243. Z733.U57I6, v. 17

Quotes passage describing the scene at the Capitol on Mar. 4, 1809, from a diary kept by Sarah Ridg.

537

Presidential inaugurations: Madison–1806 [sic] Ladies' magazine and literary gazette, v. 4, Dec. 1831: 529-537. AP2.A343, v. 4

538

Smith, Abbot E. James Madison: builder; a new estimate of a memorable career. New York, Wilson-Erickson, 1937. 366 p. plates, ports.
E342.S55

First inauguration: p. 274-275.

James Madison
Second Inauguration

539

Brant, Irving. James Madison. v. 6. Commander in Chief, 1812-1836. Indianapolis, Bobbs-Merrill [1961] 627 p. facsims., plates, ports.
E342.B7, v. 6

Second inauguration: p. 149-151.

540

The President's speech [text]. Weekly register, v. 4, Mar. 6, 1813: 15-16.
JK1.N5, v. 4

James Monroe

541

Barbee, David R. Clay peevishness caused first outdoor inaugural. *In* The Washington post. Inaugural edition, Saturday, March 4, 1933. Washington, 1933. p. 10. E806.W28

542

Barbee, David R. Monroe inaugural plan altered late; quarrel in Congress gained public chance to view "swearing in." *In* The Washington post. Inaugural edition, Saturday, March 4, 1933. Washington, 1933. p. 18. E806.W28

543

Burton, Harold H., *and* Thomas E. Waggaman. [First outdoor inaugural ceremony] *In* Columbia Historical Society, *Washington, D.C.* Records. v. 51/52; 1951-52. Washington, 1955. p. 143-144.
F191.C72, v. 51-52

In their article, "The Story of the Place."
Concerns the inauguration of Monroe on Mar. 4, 1817.

544

Cresson, William P. James Monroe. Chapel Hill, University of North Carolina Press [1946] xiv, 577 p. facsims., plates, ports. E372.C7

First inauguration: p. 281-283.

Second inauguration: p. 354-356.
Inauguration of J. Q. Adams: p. 470-471.

545
Hoyt, Edwin P. James Monroe. Chicago, Reilly & Lee Co. [1968] 127 p. illus., map, ports. E372.H6

First inauguration: p. 61-62.

546
The inauguration. Niles' weekly register, v. 12, Mar. 8, 1817: 17-20. JK1.N5, v. 12

Includes text of inaugural address.

547
Monroe inaugurated one hundred years ago today. Sunday star (Washington), Mar. 4, 1917, pt. 4: 4. illus. Newsp

548
Morgan, George. The life of James Monroe. Boston, Small, Maynard [c1921] xvi, 484 p. plates, ports. E372.M84

First inauguration: p. 351-353.
Second inauguration: p. 385-387.

549
Smith, Ira L. How inaugurations came into the open: forty red chairs, center of argument between Henry Clay and group of Senators in 1817, played major part in ending early practice of holding the ceremonies indoors. Sunday star (Washington), Mar. 5, 1933, pt. 7: 12, 23. illus. Newsp

550
Wood, Walter. Clay's dispute with Senators started outdoor inaugurals. Evening star (Washington), Jan. 20, 1953, special inaugural rotogravure section: 3. illus. Newsp

James Monroe
Second Inauguration

551
Inaugural speech [text]. Niles' weekly register, v. 20, Mar. 10, 1821: 17-21. JK1.N5, v. 20

John Quincy Adams

552

Barbee, David R. Gala inauguration for second Adams. *In* The Washington post. Inaugural edition, Saturday, March 4, 1933. Washington, 1933. p. 8. E806.W28

553

Barbee, David R. J. Q. Adams tells of own inaugural; sixth President author of concise account of what happened. *In* The Washington post. Inaugural edition, Saturday, March 4, 1933. Washington, 1933. p. 2. E806.W28

554

Bemis, Samuel Flagg. John Quincy Adams and the Union. New York, Knopf, 1956. xix, 546 p. illus., ports. E377.B46

Inauguration: p. 51-53.
Jackson's inauguration: p. 152-153.

555

Inaugural address [text]. Niles' weekly register, v. 28, Mar. 5, 1825: 8-11. JK1.N5, v. 28

556

The inauguration. Niles' weekly register, v. 28, Mar. 12, 1825: 19-20. JK1.N5, v. 28

"From the National Intelligencer of March 5."

557

Inauguration of President. *In* The American annual register. v. 1; 1825/26. New York, G. & C. Carvill, 1827. p. 29-36. D2.A5, v. 1

Includes text of inaugural address.

558

Seward, William H. Life and public services of John Quincy Adams, sixth President of the United States. Auburn [N.Y.], Derby, Miller, 1849. 404 p. port. E377.S51

Inauguration and inaugural address: p. 150-160.

Andrew Jackson

559

Barbee, David R. Mob inaugurated Andrew Jackson; General walked to Capitol and rode to White House, afterward wrecked. *In* The

Washington post. Inaugural edition, Saturday, March 4, 1933. Washington, 1933. p. 13. E806.W28

560

Bassett, John S. The life of Andrew Jackson. New ed. New York, Macmillan, 1931. 2 v. in 1 (xix, 766 p.) illus., maps, ports.
E382.B35

Inauguration: p. 421-431.

561

Goodwin, Philo A. Biography of Andrew Jackson, President of the United States. Hartford, Clapp and Benton, 1832. 456 p. plates, port.
E382.G65 1832

First inauguration: p. 315-320.

562

[Inaugural address] *In* The American annual register. v. 5; 1829/30. Boston, Gray and Bowen, 1832. p. 14-16. D2.A5, v. 5

563

The inauguration. Niles' weekly register, v. 36, Mar. 7, 1829: 28-29.
JK1.N5, v. 36

Includes text of inaugural address.

564

James, Marquis. The life of Andrew Jackson, complete in one volume. Indianapolis, Bobbs-Merrill [c1938] 972 p. facsims., maps, plates, ports.
E382.J28

First inauguration: p. 493-495.
Second inauguration: p. 624.
Van Buren's inauguration: p. 719-720.

565

Lorant, Stefan. Gobbled the drinks: noisy 'rabble' made Jackson ceremonies a rowdy affair. Times-herald (Washington), Jan. 18, 1949: 1, 15. Newsp

566

Ogg, Frederic A. The reign of Andrew Jackson; a chronicle of the frontier in politics. New Haven, Yale University Press, 1919. 249 p. illus. (The Chronicles of America series, v. 20) E381.O34

First inauguration: p. 119-124.

567

Parton, James. Life of Andrew Jackson. New York, Mason Bros., 1860. 3 v. facsims., ports. E382.P27

First inauguration: v. 3, p. 169-172.
Van Buren's inauguration: v. 3, p. 628-629.

568

Presidential inaugurations: Jackson—1829. Ladies' magazine and literary gazette, v. 5, Mar. 1832: 112-117. AP2.A343, v. 5

569

Smith, Margaret (Bayard). Andrew Jackson is inaugurated. *In* Commager, Henry S., *ed.* Living ideas in America. New York, Harper [1951] p. 173-176. E173.C67

Also published, with slightly different title and introductory remarks, in *The Heritage of America,* edited by Henry S. Commager and Allan Nevins, rev. and enl. ed. (Boston, Little, Brown, 1949. E178.C7274), p. 611-616.

570

Stevenson, Victoria F. 1929 inaugural period is centenary of Old Hickory's triumph. Sunday star (Washington), Mar. 3, 1929, pt. 7: 2. port. Newsp

Andrew Jackson
Second Inauguration

571

Hone, Philip. The diary of Philip Hone, 1828-1851. Edited, with an introduction by Allan Nevins. New York, Dodd, Mead, 1927. 2 v. ports. F128.44.H78

Jackson's second inauguration: v. 1, p. 88-89.

572

The inauguration. Niles' weekly register, v. 44, Mar. 9, 1833: 21-22. JK1.N5, v. 44

Includes text of inaugural address.

573

Washington, D.C. Inaugural Committee, *1933.* [Second inauguration of Andrew Jackson, March 4, 1833] Washington, 1933. 5 l. DWP

Press release.
In Jackson folder.

Martin Van Buren

574

Alexander, Holmes M. The American Talleyrand; the career and contemporaries of Martin Van Buren, eighth President. New York, Harper, 1935. 430 p. plates, ports. E387.A55

Inauguration: p. 333-334.

575

The inauguration. Niles' weekly register, v. 52, Mar. 11, 1837: 18-20. JK1.N5, v. 52

"From the Washington Globe." Includes text of inaugural address.

576

Lynch, Denis T. An epoch and a man, Martin Van Buren and his times. New York, H. Liveright, 1929. 566 p. plates, ports. E387.L98

Inauguration: p. 400-403.

577

Shepard, Edward M. Martin Van Buren. [Rev. ed.] Boston, Houghton Mifflin, 1899. 499 p. facsims., ports. (American statesmen, v. 18) E387.S545

Inauguration: p. 282-283.

578

U.S. *President, 1829-1837 (Jackson)* The farewell address of Andrew Jackson: and the inaugural of Martin Van Buren, President of the United States. Published and delivered on the fourth of March, one thousand eight hundred and thirty-seven. Raleigh, N.C., T. Loring, 1837. 36 p. E381.U51 Rare Bk. Coll.

579

U.S. *President, 1829-1837 (Jackson)* Farewell address of Andrew Jackson to the people of the United States: and the inaugural address of Martin Van Buren, President of the United States. Washington, Blair & Rives, 1837. 23 p. E381.U52

580

Willis, Nathaniel P. View of the Capitol at Washington. *In his* American scenery; or, Land, lake, and river, illustrations of transatlantic nature. v. 1. London, G. Virtue, 1840. p. 36-38. map, plates.
E165.W73, v. 1

Mainly an account of Van Buren's inauguration.

William Henry Harrison

581

Barbee, David R. Inauguration of Gen. Henry Harrison colorful affair but highly riotous. *In* The Washington post. Inaugural edition, Saturday, March 4, 1933. Washington, 1933. p. 7. E806.W28

582

Cleaves, Freeman. Old Tippecanoe; William Henry Harrison and his time. New York, C. Scribner's Sons, 1939. xiv, 422 p. facsims., maps, plates, ports. E392.C64

Inauguration: p. 336-338.

583

Goebel, Dorothy (Burne). William Henry Harrison; a political biography. Indianapolis, Historical Bureau of the Indiana Library and Historical Dept., 1926. 456 p. (Indiana historical collections, v. 14. Biographical series, v. 2) E392.G58

Published also as thesis (Ph.D.), Columbia University, 1926.
Inauguration: p. 370-374.

584

Grattan, Thomas C. Inauguration of President Harrison. *In his* Civilized America. v. 1. London, Bradbury and Evans, 1859. p. 337-344.
E166.G81, v. 1

585

Green, James A. William Henry Harrison, his life and times. Richmond, Garrett and Massie [1941] 536 p. plates, ports. E392.G8

Inauguration: p. 391-393.

586

Harvey, Peter. Mr. Webster kills seventeen Roman proconsuls. *In* Commager, Henry S., *and* Allan Nevins, *eds.* The heritage of America. Rev. and enl. ed. Boston, Little, Brown, 1949. p. 621-623. E178.C7274

Story of Webster's editorial work on W. H. Harrison's inaugural address, first published in Harvey's *Reminiscences and Anecdotes of Daniel Webster* (Boston, Little, Brown, 1882. E340.W4H3 1882), p. 160-163.

587

The inaugural address [text]. Niles' national register, v. 60, Mar. 6, 1841: 1-4. JK1.N5, v. 60

588

The inauguration. Niles' national register, v. 60, Mar. 13, 1841: 18-19. JK1.N5, v. 60

"From the National Intelligencer."

589

[Inauguration ceremonies]. Congressional globe, 26th Congress, 2d session, v. 9, Mar. 4, 1841: 232-235. J11.G5, v. 9

590

U.S. *Congress. Senate. Committee of Arrangements for the Inauguration, 1841.* Arrangements for the inauguration of the President elect, on the 4th of March, 1841. [Washington, 1841] 3 p. Mss

In U.S. Miscellany, Executive Mansion.

591

Washington twenty years ago. Inauguration of President Harrison. Leisure hour, v. 10, Apr. 4, 1861: 215-216, 218. AP4.L4, v. 10

592

Wolcott, John D. A Washington tragedy of a century ago; the brief administration of President William Henry Harrison. *In* Sons of the American Revolution. *District of Columbia Society.* Year book of the golden anniversary of the society, 1890-1940. Washington, 1941. p. 26-29. E202.3.D77 1940

John Tyler

593

Life of John Tyler, President of the United States, up to the close of the second session of the Twenty-seventh Congress. New York, Harper, 1843. 256 p. port. E397.L72

Inauguration and address: p. 183-186.

594

Morgan, Robert J. A Whig embattled; the Presidency under John Tyler. Lincoln, University of Nebraska Press, 1954. 199 p. port.
E396.M6

Inauguration and address: p. 7-9, 18-21.

595

The new President. Niles' national register, v. 60, Apr. 10, 1841: 87.
JK1.N5, v. 60

596

Seager, Robert. And Tyler too; a biography of John and Julia Gardiner Tyler. New York, McGraw-Hill Book Co. [1963] xvii, 681 p.
E397.S4

W. H. Harrison's inauguration: p. 144.
Tyler's succession and swearing in: p. 147-149.

597

Tyler, Lyon G. The letters and times of the Tylers. Richmond, Whittet & Shepperson, 1884-96. 3 v. facsims., plates, ports. E397.T98

Vol. 3, published Williamsburg, Va., 1896, is a supplement.
Inauguration: v. 2, p. 11-13.

James Knox Polk

598

Barbee, David R. Polk inaugural was "respectable"; event of 1845 in marked contrast with Jackson entry into office. *In* The Washington post. Inaugural edition, Saturday, March 4, 1933. Washington, 1933. p. 17.
E806.W28

599

Barbee, David R. Rainstorm greeted Polk; led to death; early President almost succumbed on his journey back home. *In* The Washington post. Inaugural edition, Saturday, March 4, 1933. Washington, 1933. p. 6.
E806.W28

600

[Inauguration ceremonies]. Congressional globe, 28th Congress, 2d session, v. 14, Mar. 4, 1845: 398-400. J11.G5, v. 14

601
Inauguration of President Polk. Inaugural address [text]. Niles' national register, v. 68, Mar. 8, 1845: 1-3. JK1.N5, v. 68

602
Inauguration of the American President. Illustrated London news, v. 6, Apr. 19, 1845: 243-244. illus. AP4.I3, v. 6

603
Jenkins, John S. James Knox Polk, and a history of his administration. Auburn, J. M. Alden, 1851. xv, 395 p. port. E417.J522

Inauguration and address: p. 145-160.

604
Morrel, Martha M. "Young Hickory," the life and times of President James K. Polk. New York, E. P. Dutton, 1949. 381 p. ports. E417.M67

Inauguration: p. 245-249.
Taylor's inauguration: p. 345-346.

605
One hundred years ago: reproductions and quotations from "The Illustrated London News" of April 19, 1845. Illustrated London news, v. 206, Apr. 21, 1945: 418. illus. AP4.I3, v. 206

606
Polk comes in little known public figure; news of arrival in Washington for inauguration first to be flashed to Nation by wire. Washington herald, Mar. 4, 1933: 4-B. Newsp

607
Sellers, Charles G. James K. Polk, continentalist, 1843-1846. Princeton, N.J., Princeton University Press, 1966. 513 p. illus., ports. E417.S4

Inauguration: p. 208-211.

608
Severn, William. Frontier President: James K. Polk. New York, I. Washburn [1965] 219 p. E417.S47

Inauguration: p. 153-155.
Taylor's inauguration: p. 210.

Zachary Taylor

609

Barbee, David R. Taylor loudly acclaimed in journey to Washington. *In* The Washington post. Inaugural edition, Saturday, March 4, 1933. Washington, 1933. p. 16. E806.W28

610

Dyer, Brainerd. Zachary Taylor. Baton Rouge, Louisiana State University Press, 1946. 455 p. maps, plan, plates, ports. (Southern biography series) E422.D995

Inauguration: p. 307-309.

611

Hamilton, Holman. Zachary Taylor. [v. 2] Soldier in the White House. Indianapolis, Bobbs-Merrill [1951] 496 p. illus., facsims., maps, ports. E422.H3, v. 2

Inauguration: p. 154-161.
Swearing in of Fillmore: p. 393-394.

612

Howard, Oliver O. General Taylor. New York, D. Appleton, 1892. 386 p. maps, plans, port. (Great commanders) Micro 8222 E

Inauguration and address: p. 315-323.

613

Hoyt, Edwin P. Zachary Taylor. Chicago, Reilly & Lee Co. [1966] 162 p. illus., ports. (President series) E422.H87

Inauguration: p. 116-117.

614

Inaugural address [text]. Niles' national register, v. 75, Mar. 7, 1849: 150. JK1.N5, v. 75

615

The inauguration. Niles' national register, v. 75, Mar. 14, 1849: 161-163. JK1.N5, v. 75

"From the National Intelligencer."

616

[Inauguration ceremonies]. Congressional globe, 31st Congress, special session of the Senate, v. 18, appendix, Mar. 5, 1849: 326-327. J11.G5, v. 18

617

McKinley, Silas B., *and* Silas Bent. Old Rough and Ready, the life and times of Zachary Taylor. New York, Vanguard Press [1946] 329 p. E422.M15

Inauguration and address: p. 225-229.

618

Montgomery, Henry. The life of Major General Zachary Taylor, twelfth President of the United States. 20th ed., rev. and enl. Auburn, Derby, Miller, 1851. 463 p. plates, ports. E422.M786

Inauguration and address: p. 406-410.

619

Polk, James K., *Pres. U.S.* Polk; the diary of a President, 1845-1849. Edited by Allan Nevins. London, New York, Longmans, Green, 1952. xxxiv, 412 p. E416.P77 1952

"A selection from *The Diary of James K. Polk During His Presidency, 1845-1849,* edited and annotated by Milo Milton Quaife."

Taylor's inauguration: p. 388-390.

620

Tuckerman, Henry T. The inauguration. Southern literary messenger, v. 15, Apr. 1849: 236-240. AP2.S82, v. 15

Reprinted in his *The Optimist* (New York, G. P. Putnam, 1850. PS3107.O6), p. 212-223.

621

U.S. *Congress. Senate. Committee of Arrangements for the Inauguration, 1849.* Arrangements for the inauguration of the President elect, on the 5th of March, 1849. [Washington, 1849] 3 p. Mss

In Zachary Taylor Papers, ser. 2, v. 2, ac. 3891.

622

U.S. *President, 1849-1850 (Taylor)* President Taylor's inaugural address, Washington, Monday, March 4, 1849. [Washington] Towers, printer [1849] 4 p. Rare Bk. Coll.

Broadside portfolio 199, no. 19c.

325-882 O-69—7

Millard Fillmore

623

Chamberlain, Ivory. Biography of Millard Fillmore. Buffalo, Thomas & Lathrops, 1856. xv, 215 p. port. E427.C44

Inauguration: p. 125-128.

624

Griffis, William E. Millard Fillmore, constructive statesman, defender of the Constitution, President of the United States. Ithaca, N.Y., Andrus & Church [c1915] 159 p. E427.G85

Inauguration: p. 53-55.
Pierce's inauguration: p. 127.

625

Rayback, Robert J. Millard Fillmore; biography of a President. Buffalo, Published for the Buffalo Historical Society by H. Stewart, 1959. xiv, 470 p. plates, ports. (Publications of the Buffalo Historical Society, v. 40) F129.B8B88, v. 40

Taylor's inauguration: p. 196-199.
Fillmore's inauguration: p. 241.
Pierce's inauguration: p. 372-374.

Franklin Pierce

626

Barbee, David R. First inauguration pictures made in 1853. *In* The Washington post. Inaugural edition, Saturday, March 4, 1933. Washington, 1933. p. 14. E806.W28

627

Barbee, David R. Inauguration of Pierce marred by jobless parade; unemployed roughly handled by populace as they attempted counter demonstration; regular procession notable despite snow. *In* The Washington post. Inaugural edition, Saturday, March 4, 1933. Washington, 1933. p. 3. E806.W28

628

The inauguration. Illustrated news, v. 1, Mar. 12, 1853: 166. AP2.I3652, v. 1

Includes text of inaugural address. Illustrations on p. 164, 165, 168-169. Note also brief comment on p. 161.

629

Inauguration ceremonies. Congressional globe, 32d Congress, 3d session, v. 22, Mar. 4, 1853: 243-245. J11.G5, v. 22

630

The inauguration of President Pierce. Illustrated London news, v. 22, Mar. 26, 1853: 227-228. AP4.I3, v. 22

631

Nichols, Roy F. Franklin Pierce, Young Hickory of the Granite Hills. [2d ed., completely rev.] Philadelphia, University of Pennsylvania Press [1958] xvii, 625 p. facsims., maps, ports. E432.N63 1958

Inauguration: p. 234-226.
Buchanan's inauguration: p. 502.

632

Washington City. Gleason's pictorial drawing-room companion, v. 4, Mar. 26, 1853: 200, 207. illus. AP2.B227, v. 4

One picture shows Pennsylvania Avenue "with a view of the procession on the day of inauguration."

James Buchanan

633

Barbee, David R. Buchanan escaped two arsenic plots. *In* The Washington post. Inaugural edition, Saturday, March 4, 1933. Washington, 1933. p. 19. E806.W28

634

Curtis, George T. Life of James Buchanan, fifteenth President of the United States. New York, Harper, 1883. 2 v. ports. E437.C98

Inauguration: v. 2, p. 187-193.

635

[Inauguration ceremonies]. Congressional globe, 35th Congress, special session of the Senate, v. 26, Mar. 4, 1857: 371-372. J11.G5, v. 26

636

Inauguration of Mr. Buchanan as President of the United States. Illustrated London news, v. 30, Mar. 28, 1857: 295-296. illus. AP4.I3, v. 30

637

The inauguration of President Buchanan; administration of the oath. Frank Leslie's illustrated newspaper, v. 3, Mar. 14, 1857: 223.
AP2.L52, v. 3

Illustrations on p. 217, 224, 225. Additional illustrations in the issue of Mar. 21 on p. 237, 240, 245.

638

Klein, Philip S. President James Buchanan, a biography. University Park, Pennsylvania State University Press [1962] xviii, 506 p. illus., ports.
E437.K53

Inauguration: p. 269-272.
Lincoln's first inauguration: p. 402.

639

One hundredth anniversary of the inauguration of James Buchanan. Congressional record, 85th Congress, 1st session, v. 103, Mar. 4, 1957: 2967-2969.
J11.R5, v. 103

Includes a long excerpt from a paper read by Dr. Homer T. Rosenberger to the Columbia Historical Society about the inauguration of President Buchanan.

640

Stern, Philip Van Doren. First photograph of an inauguration. Parade, Jan. 20, 1957: 2.
AP2.P263, 1957

Shows scene at Buchanan's inauguration.

641

U.S. *Congress. Joint Committee of Arrangements for the Inauguration, 1857.* Arrangements for the inauguration of the President elect on the fourth of March, 1857. [Washington, 1857] [4] p. plan.
Mss

In U.S. Miscellany, Executive Mansion.

642

U.S. *President, 1857-1861 (Buchanan)* Inaugural address of the President of the United States, on the fourth of March, 1857. Washington, A. O. P. Nicholson, 1857. 9 p.
E436.U575

643

Windle, Mary J. Fourth of March–inaugural of Mr. Buchanan. *In her* Life in Washington, and life here and there. Philadelphia, J. B. Lippincott, 1859. p. 96-102.
F198.W76

Abraham Lincoln

644

Adams, Charles Francis. [Lincoln's first inauguration] *In* Massachusetts Historical Society, *Boston.* Proceedings. v. 42; 1908/09. Boston, 1909. p. 148-151. F61.M38, v. 42

645

Aldrich, Charles. At Lincoln's first inauguration. Annals of Iowa, 3d ser., v. 8, Apr. 1907: 43-50. F616.A6, 3d s., v. 8

646

Barbee, David R. Washington armed at Lincoln's first; assassination of President-elect was feared and guarded against. *In* The Washington post. Inaugural edition, Saturday, March 4, 1933. Washington, 1933. p. 5. E806.W28

647

Canby, Courtlandt, *ed.* Lincoln and the Civil War; a profile and a history. New York, G. Braziller, 1960. 416 p. E457.C2 1960

First inauguration and address: p. 52-56.
Second inauguration: p. 331-333.

648

Chittenden, Lucius E. Recollections of President Lincoln and his administration. New York, Harper, 1891. 470 p. port. E457.C54

First inauguration: p. 84-92.

649

Clark, Allen C. Abraham Lincoln in the National Capital. Washington [Press of W. F. Roberts Co.] 1925. 179 p. facsims., plates, ports. E457.C58

Lincoln at Taylor's inaugural ball: p. 8.
First inauguration: p. 11-16.
Second inauguration: p. 83-84.
Originally published in the *Records* of the Columbia Historical Society (F191.C72), v. 27, 1925, p. 1-174.

650

Classman, Don. When Lincoln took oath; country's most dramatic inaugural. Sunday star (Washington), Feb. 10, 1929, pt. 7: 1, 6. illus. Newsp

651

The diary of a public man; an intimate view of the national administration, December 28, 1860, to March 15, 1861; and A page of political correspondence, Stanton to Buchanan; prefatory notes by F. Lauriston Bullard; foreword by Carl Sandburg. Chicago, Priv. print. for Abraham Lincoln Book Shop, 1945. 117 p. facsims., ports. D440.5.D55

The anonymous diary was first published in *The North American Review* (AP2.N7), v. 129, Aug.-Nov. 1879.

Lincoln's first inauguration: p. 72-80. The authenticity of detail in this account has been questioned by some scholars.

652

Grigg, William. Ceremony pleases Sandburg: 20,000 see Lincoln re-enactment. Evening star (Washington), Mar. 5, 1961: B-1. illus. Newsp

653

Hall, Abraham Oakey. The great Lincoln inauguration. Frank Leslie's popular monthly, v. 43, Mar. 1897: 254-260. illus. AP2.A346, v. 43

654

Hubbell, Jay B. Lincoln's first inaugural address. American historical review, v. 36, Apr. 1931: 550-552. E171.A57, v. 36

655

The inauguration. Harper's weekly, v. 5, Mar. 16, 1861: 165-166. illus. AP2.H32, v. 5

Illustrations on p. 161, 168-169, 176. Notes on the inaugural of the Vice President and on the inaugural ball appear on p. 167.

656

Inauguration ceremonies. Congressional globe, 37th Congress, special session of the Senate, v. 30, Mar. 4, 1861: 1433-1435. J11.G5, v. 30

657

Inauguration day, March 4, 1861. A young Detroit girl's witness to the stirring events in the city of Washington on the day of Abraham Lincoln's first inauguration as revealed in a letter to her sisters. An A.L.s. from the Burton Historical Collection of the Detroit Public

Library, with an introduction and notes by M. Garnett McCoy. Detroit, Friends of the Detroit Public Library, 1960. 13 p. facsims.
Rare Bk. Coll.

In the Stern Collection.

658

The inauguration of Abraham Lincoln, the sixteenth President of the United States of America. Frank Leslie's illustrated newspaper, v. 11, Mar. 16, 1861: 259. AP2.L52, v. 11

Illustrations on p. 261, 264-265, 269.

659

The inauguration of President Lincoln. Illustrated London news, v. 38, Mar. 30, 1861: 300. AP4.I3, v. 38

Illustration on p. 299.

660

Janny, W. A. Lincoln's inauguration; a letter from W. A. Janny to his friend Will Thomson. Lincoln herald, v. 54, winter 1952: 44-46.
E457.M887, v. 54

661

Kimmel, Stanley P. Mr. Lincoln's Washington. New York, Coward-McCann [1957] 224 p. illus., facsims., maps, ports. E501.K5

First inauguration: p. 22-33.
Second inauguration: p. 162-169.

662

Leech, Margaret. Reveille in Washington, 1860-1865. New York, Harper [c1941] 483 p. illus., facsims., maps, plates. E501.L4

Lincoln's inaugurations: p. 42-46, 366-372, and scattered references as indexed.

663

Lincoln, Abraham, *Pres. U.S.* Inaugural address of Abraham Lincoln, the country's martyr, delivered at his first inauguration, March 4, 1861. [Washington] R. O. Polkinhorn [1865?] broadside. 43 x 36 cm.
E457.94 1861A

664

Lincoln, Abraham, *Pres. U.S.* Inaugural address of the President of the United States on the fourth of March, 1861. [Washington?] 1861. 10 p. ([U.S.] 37th Congress, special session, 1861. Senate. Executive document no. 1) E457.94 1861c Rare Bk. Coll.

665

Lincoln, Abraham, *Pres. U.S.* Lincoln's inaugurals, the Emancipation proclamation, etc. [Boston, Directors of the Old South Work, 1896] 16 p. (Old South leaflets. [General series. v. 1] no. 11) E173.O44, v. 1

666

Lincoln, Abraham, *Pres. U.S.* President Lincoln's inaugural address. March 4, 1861. [Washington? Printed at the National Republican Office, 1861?] 4 p. E457.94 1861B Rare Bk. Coll.

667

Lincoln becomes President as U.S. faces dissolution. Washington herald, Mar. 4, 1933: 6-B. Newsp

668

Lincoln lore. no. 1+ Apr. 15, 1929+ Fort Wayne, Ind., Lincoln National Life Insurance Co. illus. E457.L74

Weekly, Apr. 15, 1929-June 25, 1956; monthly, July 1956+

Several issues deal with various aspects of Lincoln's inaugurations and inaugural addresses, as follows:

no. 47. The first inaugural. Mar. 3, 1930. 1 p.

no. 189. References to religion in the second inaugural. Lincoln's second inaugural address. Nov. 21, 1932. 1 p.

no. 203. Inaugural highlights. Feb. 27, 1933. 1 p.

no. 308. Preliminaries and aftermath of the first inaugural. Mar. 4, 1935. 1 p.

no. 358-359. Original draft of the first inaugural. Feb. 17-24, 1936. [2] p.

no. 569. Comments on the second inaugural address. Mar. 4, 1940. 1 p.

no. 623. Broadcasting Lincoln's first inaugural. Mar. 17, 1941. 1 p.

no. 777. Pamphlet printed in President's second inaugural parade. Feb. 28, 1944. 1 p.

no. 840. Lincoln's second inaugural address. May 14, 1945. 1 p.

no. 1241. Lincoln's first inaugural–miscellany. Jan. 19, 1953. 1 p.

no. 1243. Lincoln's first inaugural–pro and con. Feb. 2, 1953. 1 p.
no. 1404. The Queen, the Emperor, the President, 1861. Mar. 5, 1956. 1 p.
no. 1427. The inauguration of Abraham Lincoln, March 4, 1861. Jan. 1957: 1-2, 4. illus.
no. 1452-1453. Lincoln's second inaugural, a gala event in Washington society. Feb. 1959: 1-3; Mar.: 1-4. illus.
no. 1477. Chronicle junior. Mar. 1961: 1-4. facsim.

669

Lorant, Stefan. Clouds across the Potomac: riflemen hidden on rooftops guarded Lincoln's parade line. Times-herald (Washington), Jan. 19, 1949: 1, 15. Newsp

670

Lorant, Stefan. Lincoln, a picture story of his life. Rev. and enl. ed. New York, Harper [1957] 304 p. illus., facsims., ports. E457.6.L78 1957

First inauguration: p. 114-117.
Second inauguration: p. 226-231.

671

Mitgang, Herbert, *ed.* Lincoln as they saw him. New York, Rinehart [1956] 519 p. illus., ports. E457.15.M5

First inauguration and comments on address: p. 235-242.
Second inauguration: p. 434-438.

672

Nevins, Allan. The emergence of Lincoln. v. 2. Prologue to civil war, 1859-1861. New York, Scribner, 1950. 524 p. illus., maps, ports. E415.7.N38

First inauguration: p. 457-461.

673

Nevins, Allan. He did hold Lincoln's hat. American heritage, v. 10, Feb. 1959: 98-99. port. E171.A43, v. 10

Cities contemporary newspaper account verifying incident involving Sen. Stephen A. Douglas.

674

Nicolay, John G., *and* John Hay. Abraham Lincoln: a history. Lincoln's inauguration. Century magazine, v. 35, Dec. 1887: 265-284. illus.
AP2.C4, v. 35

675

The 100th anniversary of the inaugural of Abraham Lincoln. Extension of remarks of Hon. Fred Schwengel, of Iowa, in the House of Representatives, Thursday, March 9, 1961. Congressional record, 87th Congress, 1st session, v. 107: 3688-3691. J11.R5, v. 107

676

Randall, James G. Lincoln the President. New York, Dodd, Mead, 1945-55. 4 v. illus., facsims., maps, ports. (American political leaders)
E457.R2

First inauguration and address: v. 1, p. 293-310.

Second inauguration: v. 4, p. 341-344.

Similar information appears in the author's *Mr. Lincoln,* edited by Richard N. Current (New York, Dodd, Mead, 1957. 392 p. illus. E457.R215), on p. 139-142 and p. 337-340.

677

Raymond, Henry J. The life and public services of Abraham Lincoln. To which are added anecdotes and personal reminiscences of President Lincoln, by Frank B. Carpenter. New York, Derby and Miller, 1865. 808 p. facsims., plates, ports. E457.R265

First inauguration and address: p. 161-170.

Second inauguration and address: p. 669-671.

678

Sandburg, Carl. Abraham Lincoln; the war years. New York, Harcourt, Brace [1939] 4 v. illus., facsims., maps, plates, ports. E457.4.S36

First inauguration: v. 1, p. 120-140.

Second inauguration: v. 4, p. 85-99, 118-120.

679

Sandburg, Carl. Address, upon the occasion of Abraham Lincoln's one hundredth inaugural anniversary. East front of the United States Capitol, March 4, 1961. With an introduction by Carl Haverlin. Chicago, Black Cat Press [1961] xvi, 32 p. 67 mm.
E457.7.S32 Min. Case

680

Sat by Mrs. Lincoln: Mrs. Teall recalls inauguration day of 1861. Washington post, Mar. 4, 1905, pt. 2: 1. Newsp

681

Stepp, John W. Lincoln is inaugurated 16th President: the inaugural as reported by the Star 100 years ago. Sunday, the star magazine (Washington), Mar. 5, 1961: 4-5, 14. illus. Newsp

682

Tarbell, Ida M. The life of Abraham Lincoln, drawn from original sources and containing many speeches, letters, and telegrams hitherto unpublished. New York, Lincoln Historical Society, 1924. 4 v. illus., facsims., maps, plates, ports. E457.T184

Lincoln as one of the managers of Taylor's inaugural ball: v. 2, p. 21-22.
Prepares first inaugural address: v. 3, p. 19-21.
First inauguration and address: v. 3, p. 47-61.
Second inaugural address: v. 4, p. 60-61.

683

Thomas, Benjamin P. Abraham Lincoln, a biography. New York, Knopf, 1952. 548 p. illus., maps, ports. E457.T427 1952

First inauguration: p. 245-248.
Second inauguration: p. 503-504.

684

U.S. *Congress. Joint Committee to Commemorate the One Hundredth Anniversary of the First Inaugural of Abraham Lincoln.* Ceremonies and reenactment of the one hundredth anniversary of the first inauguration of Abraham Lincoln, 1861-1961, on the east front of the Capitol of the United States, March 4, 1961. Washington, U.S. Govt. Print. Off., 1962. xxvi, 37 p. illus. ([U.S.] 87th Congress, 2d session. House document no. 523) E457.7.U5965

685

U.S. *Congress. Senate. Committee of Arrangements for the Inauguration, 1861.* Arrangements for the inauguration of the President of the United States, on the fourth of March, 1861. [Washington? 1861] 3 p. plan. E457.U6 Rare Bk. Coll.

Copy also in the general collections (F198.W35).

686

U.S. *Lincoln Sesquicentennial Commission.* Lincoln day by day; a chronology, 1809-1865. Earl Schenck Miers, editor-in-chief. Washington, 1960. 3 v. E457.U66

Lincoln attends Taylor's inauguration and inaugural ball: v. 2, p. 9.
First inauguration: v. 3, p. 24-26.
Second inauguration: v. 3, p. 317-318.

687

U.S. *President, 1861-1865 (Lincoln)* Lincoln's inaugural and first message to Congress. New York, A. Lovell, 1894. 27 p. (American history leaflets, no. 18. Nov. 1894) E173.A66, no. 18

688

Wall, Bernhardt. Following Abraham Lincoln, 1809-1865. New York, Wise-Parslow Co. [1943] xix, 415 p. col. illus. E457.W222

First inauguration: p. 299-301.
Second inauguration: p. 387-389.

689

Wallis, G. B. Honest Abe and the Little Giant. A reminiscence of Lincoln's first inauguration. Outlook, v. 127, Feb. 9, 1921: 217-219. illus. AP2.O8, v. 127

690

Wessen, Ernest J. Lincoln's first inaugural address. Abraham Lincoln quarterly, v. 3, Mar. 1944: 34-37. E457.7.A22, v. 3

About rare editions of the speech.

691

White, Jean. Forgot to pay hotel bill: Willard looks back on '61 inaugural when guest Lincoln proved honest. Washington post, Jan. 18, 1957: A1. Newsp

Illustrations, including facsimile of letter, on p. B6.

692

White, Jean. 20,000 at re-enacted inaugural hear Sandburg echo Lincoln. Washington post, Mar. 5, 1961: A-1. illus. Newsp

Other illustrations on p. B-1.

Abraham Lincoln
Second Inauguration

693

Attorney recalls Lincoln's inaugural 72 years ago. James F. Duhamel watched parade from father's carriage. Evening star (Washington), Jan. 12, 1937: B-1. port. Newsp

694

Barbee, David R. Lincoln's second drab and stormy; terrible crush at Capitol when inauguration was moved outdoors. *In* The Washington post. Inaugural edition, Saturday, March 4, 1933. Washington, 1933. p. 5. E806.W28

695

Bishop, James A. The day Lincoln was shot. With illustrations selected and arranged by Stefan Lorant. New York, Harper [1955] 304 p. illus., map, ports. E457.5.B63

Lincoln's second inauguration: p. 34-37.

696

Brooks, Noah. Lincoln's second inauguration. *In his* Washington in Lincoln's time. New York, Century Co., 1895. p. 235-241. E501.B87

697

Chambrun, Charles Adolphe de Pineton, *marquis* de. Impressions of Lincoln and the Civil War, a foreigner's account; translated from the French by Aldebert de Chambrun. New York, Random House [1952] 174 p. illus. E457.15.C45

The author's letters to his wife from Dec. 20, 1864, to June 13, 1865.

Lincoln's second inauguration: p. 34-40.

698

Chronicle junior. Printed in the inauguration procession of Lincoln & Johnson. Washington, D.C., March 4th, 1865. 4 p. Mss

Contains "An Inaugural Poem, Dedicated to Abraham Lincoln, of Illinois, and Andrew Johnson, of Tennessee" (p. 1; printed in red ink); an editiorial, "The Reinauguration To-day" (p. 2; printed in blue ink); and "Inauguration Programme" (p. 3-4; printed in black ink).

Accompanied by a copy of the first page only, printed in red ink on silk, for President Lincoln.

In the Robert Todd Lincoln Collection of the Papers of Abraham Lincoln, v. 191.

699

Commemoration ceremony of the 100th anniversary of the 2d inauguration of Abraham Lincoln, 1865-1965, Mar. 4, 1965, on the east front of the Capitol, City of Washington, Hon. Melvin Price, chairman. Congressional record, 89th Congress, 1st session, v. 111: 4240-4245.
J11.R5, v. 111

700

Dewar, Helen. 'With malice toward none': Lincoln inaugural evoked. Washington post, Mar. 5, 1965: C-1. illus. Newsp

701

Douglass, Frederick. Life and times. Centenary memorial subscribers' ed. New York, Pathway Press [c1941] 695 (*i.e.* 703) p. illus., plates.
E449.D744 1941

"Substantially a reproduction of the text of the last revised and complete work" (published in 1893).

Lincoln's second inauguration and reception: p. 398-404.

702

Green, Samuel A. [The Lincoln inaugural table] *In* Massachusetts Historical Society, *Boston.* Proceedings. v. 42; 1908/09. Boston, 1909. p. 135. illus. F61.M38, v. 42

Describes and pictures an iron table "which stood in front of Lincoln when he delivered his second inaugural message in Washington on March 4, 1865; and was given to the Society by Benjamin B. French on October 11, 1866."

703

Inauguration ceremonies. Congressional globe, 39th Congress, special session of the Senate, v. 35, Mar. 4, 1865: 1424-1425.
J11.G5, v. 35

704

Kunhardt, Dorothy (Meserve), *and* Philip B. Kunhardt. Twenty days; a narrative in text and pictures of the assassination of Abraham Lincoln and the twenty days and nights that followed–the Nation in mourning, the long trip home to Springfield. New York, Harper & Row [1965] 312 p. illus., facsims., ports. E457.5.K8

On p. 32-35 the authors demonstrate, by close examination of a photograph made at Lincoln's second inauguration, that John Wilkes Booth and his conspirators were at the scene, a few feet from the President.

The swearing in of President Johnson is touched on (p. [68], 103, 108).

705

Lincoln, Abraham, *Pres. U.S.* Inaugural address. March 4, 1865. [Washington? 1865] 3 p. E457.94 1865 Rare Bk. Coll.

706

McFarland, B. S. An incident. Industrialist, v. 26, Apr. 17, 1900: 398-400. S63.S3, v. 26

Includes a short account of Lincoln's second inauguration.

707

Mackay, Charles. Forty years' recollections of life, literature, and public affairs, from 1830 to 1870. v. 2. London, Chapman & Hall, 1877. 458 p. PR4971.M2Z5 1877

Lincoln's second inauguration: p. 438-446.

708

Moldenhawer, Julius V. The Lincoln of the second inaugural. *In* Abraham Lincoln Association, *Springfield, Ill.* Papers. v. 16; 1939. Springfield, 1940. p. 81-106. E457.8.A25, 1939

Considers Lincoln's character in terms of this famous address.

709

Morrow, Lance. Hollywood touch: Lincoln inaugural is re-enacted as 30,000 witness Capitol drama. Evening star (Washington), Mar. 5, 1965: B-1. illus. Newsp

710

No color line drawn: first appearance of Negroes in inauguration parade–Lincoln's second term; many new features and magnificent parade; Civil War was still in progress–ball held at the Patent Office. Evening star (Washington), Mar. 4, 1905, pt. 2: 7. Newsp

Chief Justice Chase administers the oath of office to President Lincoln at his second inauguration, March 4, 1865. From *Harper's Weekly*—see item 711.

711
The President's inaugural. Harper's weekly, v. 9, Mar. 18, 1865: 164.
AP2.H32, v. 9

Illustrations on p. 161, 168-169.

712
The second inauguration of President Lincoln. Frank Leslie's illustrated newspaper, v. 19, Mar. 18, 1865: 403. AP2.L52, v. 19

Illustration on p. 408-409.

713
Sherwood, Isaac R. I saw Lincoln inaugurated. Leslie's, v. 132, Mar. 5, 1921: 261, 285. illus. AP2.L52, v. 132

714
Stern, Philip Van Doren. "The President came forward and the sun burst through the clouds." American heritage, v. 9, Feb. 1958: 10-15, 94-97. illus. E171.A43, v. 9

A more extensive version was published as the first chapter in his *An End to Valor; the Last Days of the Civil War* (Boston, Houghton Mifflin, 1958. E477.6.S8), p. 1-28.

715
Thomson, Peggy. Men have century-long remembered the second inaugural of Lincoln, March 4, 1865. Washington post Potomac, Feb. 28, 1965: 5, 7-10. illus. Newsp

716
U.S. *Congress. Joint Committee to Commemorate the Hundredth Anniversary of the Second Inaugural of Abraham Lincoln.* Commemoration ceremony upon the occasion of the one hundredth anniversary of the second inauguration of Abraham Lincoln, 1865-1965, East Front of the United States Capitol at twelve o'clock noon, Washington, D.C., March 4, 1965. [Washington? 1965] 24 p. illus.
E457.7.U5966 Rare Bk. Coll.

717
U.S. *Congress. Senate. Committee of Arrangements for the Inauguration, 1865.* Arrangements for the inauguration of the President of the United States, on the fourth of March, 1865. Washington, Govt. Print. Off., 1865. 6 p. JK538.1865.A3

325-882 O-69—8

718

Whitman, Walt. Specimen days in America. London, H. Milford, Oxford University Press [1932] xiv, 317 p. (The World's classics, no. 371)
PS3220.A1 1932

Lincoln's second inauguration: p. 93-94, 96. Inaugural ball: p. 97.

Andrew Johnson

719

Andrew Johnson's inauguration. Frank Leslie's illustrated newspaper, v. 21, Jan. 6, 1866: 244-245. illus. AP2.L52, v. 21

720

Bowers, Claude G. The tragic era; the revolution after Lincoln. Cambridge, Houghton Mifflin Co., 1929. xxii, 567 p. facsims., plates, ports.
E668.B779

Inauguration: p. 3-4.

721

Foster, Lillian, *comp.* Andrew Johnson, President of the United States; his life and speeches. New York, Richardson, 1866. 316 p. E667.F7

Inauguration and address: p. 193-194.

722

Savage, John. The life and public services of Andrew Johnson, seventeenth President of the United States, including his state papers, speeches, and addresses. New York, Derby & Miller, 1866. 408, 130, 19 p. plates, port. E667.S26

Inauguration and address: p. 327-329.

723

Severn, William. In Lincoln's footsteps; the life of Andrew Johnson. New York, I. Washburn [1966] 215 p. illus. E667.S48

Inauguration: p. 123-124.

724

Stryker, Lloyd P. Andrew Johnson; a study in courage. New York, Macmillan Co., 1929. xvi, 881 p. illus., facsims., plates, ports.
E667.S92

Inauguration: p. 194-197.

725

Tappan, George L. Andrew Johnson–not guilty. New York, Comet Press Books [1954] 139 p. E667.T3

Inauguration: p. 85.

726

Winston, Robert W. Andrew Johnson, plebeian and patriot. New York, H. Holt [c1928] xvi, 549 p. facsims., map, plates, ports. E667.W78

Inauguration: p. 268-269.

Ulysses S. Grant

727

Badeau, Adam. Grant in peace, from Appomattox to Mount McGregor; a personal memoir. Hartford, S. S. Scranton, 1887. 591 p. illus., facsims., plates. E672.B131

First inauguration: p. 159-160.
Hayes' inauguration: p. 251-252.

728

Barbee, David R. Organized groups marched for Grant; feud with Johnson caused much comment among papers of period. *In* The Washington post. Inaugural edition, Saturday, March 4, 1933. Washington, 1933. p. 17. E806.W28

729

Briggs, Emily E. President Grant's inaugural. *In her* The Olivia letters; being some history of Washington City for forty years as told by the letters of a newspaper correspondent. New York, Neale Pub. Co., 1906. p. 95-99. F198.B85

730

Casey, Emma (Dent). Tells of the two inaugurations of President Grant. Sunday star (Washington), Mar. 4, 1917, pt. 4: 1. port. Newsp

731

Frost, Lawrence A. U. S. Grant album; a pictorial biography of Ulysses S. Grant, from leather clerk to the White House. Seattle, Superior Pub. Co. [1966] 192 p. illus., facsims., ports. E672.F76

First inauguration: p. [156].
Second inauguration: p. [164].

732
Grant's inauguration. Harper's weekly, v. 13, Mar. 20, 1869: 186.
AP2.H32, v. 13

Illustrations on p. 177, 184-185.

733
Haven, Gilbert. The national day. Independent, v. 21, Mar. 11, 1869: 1.
AP2.I53, v. 21

734
Hesseltine, William B. Ulysses S. Grant, politican. New York, Dodd, Mead, 1935. 480 p. facsims., plates, ports. (American political leaders)
E672.H46

First inauguration: p. 142-144.
Second inauguration: p. 315-317.
Hayes' inauguration: p. 422.

735
Inaugural ceremonies. [Washington] Gibson Bros. [1869] [4] p. illus., ports.
DWP

In Grant folder.

736
The inauguration. Frank Leslie's illustrated newspaper, v. 28, Mar. 20, 1869: 3.
AP2.L52, v. 28

Illustrations on p. 8-9, 12.

737
Inauguration ceremonies. Congressional globe, 41st Congress, 1st session, v. 41, Mar. 4, 1869: 1-2.
J11.G5, v. 41

738
The inauguration–to and from the Capitol. Frank Leslie's illustrated newspaper, v. 28, Mar. 27, 1869: 27.
AP2.L52, v. 28

Illustrations on p. 24, 25.

739
Military fete sways day as Grant assumes office. Washington herald, Mar. 4, 1933: 8-B.
Newsp

740

Nevins, Allan. Hamilton Fish; the inner history of the Grant administration. Rev. ed. New York, F. Ungar Pub. Co. [1957] 2 v. (xxi, 932 p.) illus., ports. E664.F52N44

Grant's first inauguration: v. 1, p. 105-107.
Grant's second inauguration: v. 2, p. 612-613.
Hayes' inauguration: v. 2, p. 857.

741

Poore, Benjamin Perley, *and* Otis H. Tiffany. Life of U. S. Grant. Philadelphia, Hubbard Bros., 1885. xxxiv, 142, 594 p. illus., ports. E672.P82

First inauguration: pt. 2, p. 42-45.
Second inauguration: pt. 2, p. 146-154.
Hayes' inauguration: pt. 2, p. 234-237.

742

Ross, Ishbel. The general's wife; the life of Mrs. Ulysses S. Grant. New York, Dodd, Mead, 1959. 372 p. illus. E672.R77

First inauguration and inaugural ball: p. 203-205.
Second inauguration and inaugural ball: p. 231-233.

743

Todd, Helen. A man named Grant. Boston, Houghton Mifflin Co., 1940. 598 p. illus. E672.T64

First inauguration: p. 388-390.
Second inauguration: p. 453-454.
Private inauguration of Hayes on Mar. 3, 1877: p. 521-523.

744

Townsend, George A. Washington, outside and inside. Hartford, Conn., J. Betts, 1873. xix, 751 p. illus. F194.T74

Grant's first inauguration: p. 679-681.

745

U.S. *Congress. Senate. Committee of Arrangements for the Inauguration, 1869.* Arrangements for the inauguration of the President of the United States, on the 4th of March, 1869. Washington, Govt. Print. Off., 1869. [4] p. F198.W352

The ball at President Grant's second inauguration. This is evidently an idealized view, for contemporary accounts speak of the icy winds which blew through the thin walls of the temporary ballroom structure, freezing the birds in the cages suspended from the ceiling and forcing dancers to retain their wraps. From *Frank Leslie's Illustrated Newspaper*—see item 751.

Ulysses S. Grant
Second Inauguration

746

U.S. *President, 1869-1877 (Grant)* Inaugural address of Ulysses S. Grant, President of the United States, March 4, 1869. Washington, Govt. Print. Off., 1869. 5 p. J82.C11 Mar. 4 Rare Bk. Coll.

747

Ames, Mary (Clemmer). Ten years in Washington. Life and scenes in the National Capital, as a woman sees them. Hartford, Conn., A. D. Worthington, 1873. xx, 587 p. F198.A51

Grant's second inauguration: p. 269-277.
Inaugural balls, 1869 and 1873: p. 278-283.

748

Ames, Mary (Clemmer). A woman's letter from Washington–inauguration day. Independent, v. 25, Mar. 13, 1873: 330-331. AP2.I53, v. 25

749

Inauguration ceremonies. Congressional record, 43d Congress, special session of the Senate, v. 1, Mar. 4, 1873: 1-2. J11.R5, v. 1

750

Lucke, Jerome B. Excursion of the Second Regiment Connecticut National Guard, to Washington, D.C., March 4, 1873. New Haven, Tuttle, Morehouse & Taylor, 1873. 48 p. F198.L94

751

President Grant's second inauguration. Frank Leslie's illustrated newspaper, v. 36, Mar. 15, 1873: 5-6. illus. AP2.L52, v. 36

Illustrations also on p. 1, 8-9, 12.
Additional illustrations were published in a supplement to the Mar. 22, 1873, issue (p. 33-36).

752

The second inauguration. Harper's weekly, v. 17, Mar. 22, 1873: 230. AP2.H32, v. 17

Illustrations on p. 220, 221, 224-225.

753

U.S. *Congress. Senate. Committee of Arrangements for the Inauguration, 1873.* Arrangements for the inauguration of the President of the

United States on the fourth of March, 1873. Washington, Govt. Print. Off., 1873. 6 p. JK538.1873.A5

754

Washington, D.C. Inauguration Committee, *1873.* [Presidential inauguration, March 4, 1873. Washington, 1873?] 2 l. DWP

Describes preparations being made by the committees, and lists their members.

In Grant folder.

Rutherford B. Hayes

755

Ames, Mary (Clemmer). A woman's letter from Washington–the inauguration. Independent, v. 29, Mar. 15, 1877: 1-2. AP2.I53, v. 29

756

Barbee, David R. Young son of Hayes wept as father won Presidency. *In* The Washington post. Inaugural edition, Saturday, March 4, 1933. Washington, 1933. p. 19. E806.W28

757

Barnard, Harry. Rutherford B. Hayes, and his America. Indianapolis, Bobbs-Merrill [1954] 606 p. illus., facsims., ports. E682.B3

Inauguration: p. 399-413.

758

Eckenrode, Hamilton J. Rutherford B. Hayes, statesman of reunion. New York, Dodd, Mead, 1930. 363 p. facsims., plates, ports. (American political leaders) E682.E19

Inauguration: p. 237-238.

759

Hayes, Rutherford B., *Pres. U.S.* Diary and letters of Rutherford Birchard Hayes, nineteenth President of the United States. Edited by Charles Richard Williams. v. 3. 1865-1881. [Columbus] Ohio State Archaeological and Historical Society, 1924. 650 p. plates, ports. (Ohio State Archaeological and Historical Society. Hayes series, v. 5) E682.H45, v. 3

Inauguration: p. 424, 426.

760
The inauguration ceremonies. Christian union, v. 15, Mar. 7, 1877: 204.
AP2.O8, v. 15

761
Inauguration ceremonies. Congressional record, 45th Congress, special session of the Senate, v. 6, Mar. 5, 1877: 2-4. J11.R5, v. 6

762
Inauguration of President Hayes and Vice-President Wheeler. Frank Leslie's illustrated newspaper, v. 44, Mar. 24, 1877: 37-38.
AP2.L52, v. 44

Illustrations on p. 33, 40, 41, 44, 45.

763
Miller, Joaquin. Inauguration of President Hayes. Frank Leslie's illustrated newspaper, v. 44, Mar. 17, 1877: 26. AP2.L52. v. 44

Poem.

764
Oath in secret gives Nation dual Presidents for a day. Washington herald, Mar. 4, 1933: 8-B. Newsp

765
Our new President. Harper's weekly, v. 21, Mar. 24, 1877: 230.
AP2.H32, v. 21

Illustrations on p. 221, 224, 228-229.

766
President Hayes. Inauguration ceremonies at the National Capital, March 5th. Frank Leslie's illustrated newspaper, v. 44, Mar. 17, 1877: 23.
AP2.L52, v. 44

Illustrations on p. 24, 25.

767
Williams, Charles R. The life of Rutherford Birchard Hayes, nineteenth President of the United States. Boston, Houghton Mifflin Co., 1914. 2 v. facsims., plates, ports. E682.W7

Inauguration: v. 2, p. 5-11.

James A. Garfield

768

Ames, Mary (Clemmer). A woman's letter from Washington. Independent, v. 33, Mar. 17, 1881: 2-3. AP2.I53, v. 33

769

Barbee, David R. Crowds acclaim Garfield despite raging blizzard; ceremony held outdoors, with new President reading his address. *In* The Washington post. Inaugural edition, Saturday, March 4, 1933. Washington, 1933. p. 15. E806.W28

770

Feis, Ruth (Stanley-Brown). Mollie Garfield in the White House. Chicago, Rand McNally [1963] 128 p. illus., ports. E687.F4

Inauguration: p. 53-58.

771

Gemmill, Jane W. Notes on Washington; or, Six years at the National Capital. Philadelphia, E. Claxton, 1884. 316 p. F199.G32

"Some of these notes were originally published in the National Republican, of Washington City."–Preface.
Inauguration of Garfield: p. 73-75.

772

The inauguration. Harper's weekly, v. 25, Mar. 19, 1881: 180. illus. AP2.H32, v. 25

Other illustrations on p. 181, 184-185.

773

Inauguration ceremonies. Congressional record, 47th Congress, special session of the Senate, v. 12, Mar. 4, 1881: 2-3. J11.R5, v. 12

774

The inauguration of President Garfield. Independent, v. 33, Mar. 10, 1881: 15. AP2.I53, v. 33

775

[Invitation to] inaugural reception & promenade concert ... at the National Museum, Washington, D.C., March 4th, 1881. New York, H. Lee Bank Note Co. [1881] 1 p. ports. DWP

Five copies in Garfield folder.

776

Keppler, Joseph. Inauguration. Puck, v. 8, Mar. 2, 1881: 438-439. col. lithograph. 28.5 x 47 cm. AP101.P7, v. 8

Caricature.

777

Lossing, Benson J. A biography of James A. Garfield. New York, H. S. Goodspeed [1882] 840 p. ports. E687.L87

Inauguration and address: p. 602-622.

778

Marchman, Watt P., *ed.* The Washington visits of Jenny Halstead, 1879-1881, from her letters. *In* Historical and Philosophical Society of Ohio. Bulletin, v. 12, July 1954: 179-193. illus. F486.H653, v. 12

In two letters dated Mar. 4 and 5, 1881 (p. 193), Miss Halstead describes briefly the inauguration of President Garfield and the ball which she attended with President and Mrs. Hayes.

779

Ogilvie, John S. The life and death of James A. Garfield, from the tow path to the White House. Cincinnati, Cincinnati Pub. Co. [1881] 457 p. facsims., plates, ports. E687.O45

Inauguration: p. 427-428.
Inauguration of Arthur: p. 441-446.

780

President Garfield's inauguration; a vast crowd and unusually brilliant spectacle. Frank Leslie's illustrated newspaper, v. 52, Mar. 19, 1881: 38-39. AP2.L52, v. 52

Illustrations on p. 33, 40-41, 44, 49, 52-53. Article includes a paragraph on the ball.

781

Ridpath, John C. The life and work of James A. Garfield, twentieth President of the United States. Memorial ed. Cincinnati, Jones Bros. [c1881] 820 p. facsims., plates, ports. E687.R56

Inauguration and address: p. 486-498.

782

Thayer, William M. From log-cabin to the White House: life of James A. Garfield. With eulogy by Hon. James G. Blaine. Enl., rev., and newly illustrated. Norwich, Conn., H. Bill Pub. Co., 1882. 483 p. plates, ports. E687.T38

Inauguration: p. 395-401.

783

U.S. *Congress. Senate. Committee of Arrangements for the Inauguration, 1881.* Arrangements for the inauguration of the President of the United States on the fourth of March, 1881. [Washington] Govt. Print. Off. [1881] [4] p. illus., plan. E687.U58

784

U.S. *President, 1881 (Garfield)* Address of James A. Garfield, on the occasion of his inauguration as President of the United States, March 4, 1881. Washington, 1881. 17 l. E686.U65 Rare Bk. Coll.

785

Washington, D.C. Inaugural Committee, *1881,* Inaugural programme, published by permission of the Executive Committee. [Washington] Gibson Bros. [1881] [16] p. illus., plan. E686.I35

In the same envelope are the following items: *Official Arrangements for the Inauguration of the President of the United States on the Fourth of March, 1881* (3 p.); *Programme, Inaugural Procession* ([3] p.); and *Official Program, Inaugural–March 4, 1881* (8 p.).

786

Wheeler, E. J. Inaugural ode, March 4th, 1881. Independent, v. 33, Mar. 10, 1881: 4. AP2.I53, v. 33

Chester A. Arthur

787

Howe, George F. Chester A. Arthur, a quarter-century of machine politics. New York, Dodd, Mead, 1934. 307 p. plates, ports. (American political leaders) E692.H67

Inauguration: p. 2, 154-156.

788

Taking the oath of office. Harper's weekly, v. 25, Oct. 1, 1881: 660. illus. AP2.H32, v. 25

789
Vice President Arthur taking the Presidential oath. Frank Leslie's illustrated newspaper, v. 53, Oct. 8, 1881: 86. AP2.L52, v. 53

Illustration on p. 81.

Grover Cleveland

790
Barbee, David R. Cleveland's first inaugural finest; 200,000 acclaim President-elect, who arrived in Capital unheralded. *In* The Washington post. Inaugural edition, Saturday, March 4, 1933. Washington, 1933. p. 9. E806.W28

791
Beard, Frank. The inauguration ball. Judge, v. 7, Mar. 7, 1885: facing p. 14. fold. col. lithograph. 42.7 x 62.5 cm. AP101.J8, v. 7

Caricature.

792
Carpenter, Frank G. Carp's Washington. Arranged and edited by Frances Carpenter. New York, McGraw-Hill [1960] 314 p. F196.C3

Cleveland's first inauguration: p. 35-38.

793
Foote, Kate. Our Washington letter. Independent, v. 37, Mar. 12, 1885: 2-3. AP2.I53, v. 37

794
The inaugural program; arrangement, order and details of the ceremonies attending the inauguration of Grover Cleveland as the 22d President of the United States at Washington, D.C., March 4, 1885. Together with a sketch of the life of the new President, his nomination, election, etc. ... Containing also brief information for the guidance of strangers visiting Washington. Washington, 1885. ICN

795
The inauguration. Christian union, v. 31, Mar. 12, 1885: 3. AP2.O8, v. 31

796
Inauguration ceremonies. Congressional record, 49th Congress, special session of the Senate, v. 17, Mar. 4, 1885: 2-3. J11.R5, v. 17

Scene near the White House on the night of President Cleveland's first inauguratio
In 1885 he took office as the first Democratic President since Buchanan, 28 years earlier. The celebrations of his inauguration were exceptionally festive and were long remembered by participants and witnesses. From *Harper's Weekly*–see item 805.

797

Kennedy, George. Inaugural parade for Cleveland recalled by oldest inhabitants. Evening star (Washington), June 5, 1947: B-13.

Newsp

798

Keppler, Joseph. Cleveland's entry into Washington, March 4th, 1885. Puck, v. 17, Mar. 4, 1885: 8-9. col. lithograph. 28.4 x 47 cm.

AP101.P7, v. 17

Caricature, "With PUCK's regards to Hans Makart and Charles V."

799

Kintz, Henry J. The inauguration of Grover Cleveland, the President-elect. March 4th, 1885. A book for fifty million people. Alexandria, Va., 1885. 159 p. plates, ports. E696.K56

800

McElroy, Robert M. Grover Cleveland, the man and the statesman; an authorized biography. New York, Harper, 1923. 2 v. ports.

E697.M14

First inauguration: v. 1, p. 110-111.
Second inauguration: v. 2, p. 9-10.
McKinley's inauguration: v. 2, p. 253-255.

801

Nevins, Allan. Grover Cleveland; a study in courage. New York, Dodd, Mead, 1932. 832 p. plates, ports. (American political leaders)

E697.N46

First inauguration: p. 206-207.

802

President Cleveland; scenes and incidents of a brilliant inauguration. Frank Leslie's illustrated newspaper, v. 60, March. 14, 1885: 54-55.

AP2.L52, v. 60

Illustrations on p. 49, 53, 56-57, 61.

803

Proctor, John C. President Cleveland's inauguration. Sunday star (Washington), May 18, 1952: C-10. Newsp

President Cleveland with his sisters, Miss Rose Cleveland at his right hand and Mrs. Hoyt behind her, receiving guests at the ball celebrating his first inauguration. From *Frank Leslie's Illustrated Newspaper*—see item 802.

804

Schreiber, Bessie R. An acrostic to President Grover Cleveland on his inauguration. Containing the names of all the newspapers in New York State. N[ew] Y[ork], H. Seibert, c1885. broadside. 45 cm. fold. to 29 x 23 cm. E696.S37

805

Townsend, George A. The inauguration. Harper's weekly, v. 29, Mar. 14, 1885: 170. AP2.H32, v. 29

Illustrations on p. 161, 164, 165. A supplement at end of this issue reproduces a double-page illustration, by T. de Thulstrup, of the inaugural ball.

806

U.S. *Congress. Senate. Committee of Arrangements for the Inauguration, 1885.* Arrangements for the inauguration of the President of the United States, on the fourth of March, 1885. [Washington, 1885] [8] p. illus., plan. JK538.1885.A5

807

Washington, D.C. Inaugural Committee, *1885.* Cleveland & Hendricks' inauguration, Mar. 4, 1885. Committees in charge of the celebration and rules for their government. Adopted by the General Committee of Fifty, December 29, 1884. [Washington, R. O. Polkinhorn [1885] 24 p. F199.W31 1885C

808

Washington, D.C. Inaugural Committee, *1885.* Final report of the Executive Committee of the inaugural ceremonies of March 4, 1885, and resolutions of the General Committee. Washington, C. W. Brown, 1885. 19 p. F199.W31 1885F

809

Washington, D.C. Military Committee, *1885.* Inauguration, 1885. [Washington, 1885] 14 p. DWP

In Cleveland 1885 folder.

Benjamin Harrison

810

Barbee, David R. Clevelands efface selves at rites; let Harrisons have all of inaugural show in March, 1889. *In* The Washington post. Inaugural edition, Saturday, March 4, 1933. Washington, 1933. p. 4. E806.W28

811

Barbee, David R. Street crowds, drenched, cheer Benjamin Harrison. *In* The Washington post. Inaugural edition, Saturday, March 4, 1933. Washington, 1933. p. 16. E806.W28

812

Boldrick, Samuel J. Writes of memories of President Harrison's inauguration. Evening star (Washington), Feb. 6, 1941: A-10. Newsp

Letter to the editor.

813

Color marked inaugurals in the early 80's. Washington herald, Mar. 14, 1929: 28. Newsp

About the inauguration of Benjamin Harrison.

814

Foote, Kate. Our Washington letter. Independent, v. 41, Mar. 14, 1889: 6-7. AP2.I53, v. 41

815

Gillam, Victor. Inauguration, March 4, 1889. Judge, v. 15, Mar. 2, 1889: 340-341. col. lithograph. 29 x 46.6 cm. AP101.J8, v. 15

Caricature of inauguration procession as medieval wedding.

816

Inauguration ceremonies. Congressional record, 51st Congress, special session of the Senate, v. 21, Mar. 4, 1889: 2-4. J11.R5, v. 21

817

Peace Monument stand. The only front views. The grand inaugural procession. Washington, R. H. Darby Print. [1889] broadside. plan. 86 x 61 cm. DWP

In Benjamin Harrison folder.

818

President Harrison's inauguration. Harper's weekly, v. 33, Mar. 16, 1889: 206. AP2.H32, v. 33

Illustrations on p. 201, 208-209.

819

Republican Party. *National Committee, 1888-1892. Executive Committee of the Inaugural Ceremonies of March 4, 1889.* Final report. Washington, Gibson Bros., 1889. 17 p. JK538.1889.R42

820

Republican Party. *National Committee, 1888-1892. Executive Committee of the Inaugural Ceremonies of March 4, 1889.* Inaugural ceremonies, March 4, 1889. Committees in charge and rules for their government adopted by the Executive Committee, November 24, 1888. [Washington] Beresford, Pr. [1888?] 30 p. DWP

In Benjamin Harrison folder.

821

Republican Party. *National Committee, 1888-1892. Executive Committee of the Inaugural Ceremonies of March 4, 1889.* Official programme of the inaugural ceremonies of President Benjamin Harrison and Vice-President Levi P. Morton, March 4th, 1889. [Washington] Fletcher & Langstaff [1889] 32 p. illus. (part col.) DWP

In Benjamin Harrison folder.

822

Sievers, Harry J. Benjamin Harrison. Chicago, H. Regnery Co., 1952-68. 3 v. illus., maps, ports. E702.S54

Vol. 2 published by University Publishers, New York, and v. 3 by Bobbs-Merrill Co., Indianapolis.

Contents. v. 1. Hoosier warrior, 1833-1865. [v. 2] Hoosier statesman: from the Civil War to the White House, 1865-1888. [v. 3] Hoosier President: the White House and after.

Inauguration: v. 1, p. 3-7; v. 3, p. 34-39.

823

Souvenir of Washington. Inauguration of Benjamin Harrison, President, and Levi P. Morton, Vice-President. Washington, Shoomaker Co. [1889] [24] p. illus. DWP

In Benjamin Harrison folder.

824

U.S. *Congress. Senate. Committee of Arrangements for the Inauguration, 1889.* Order of procession for the inauguration of the President of the

United States, on the fourth of March, 1889. [Washington] Bureau Engraving & Print. [1889] [4] p. DWP

In Benjamin Harrison folder.

825

U.S. *President, 1889-1893 (Benjamin Harrison)* Inaugural address of the President of the United States delivered March 4, 1889. Washington, Govt. Print. Off., 1889. 16 p. J82.C61 Mch. 4 Rare Bk. Coll.

Grover Cleveland
Second Inauguration

826

Bain, George G. The inauguration of President Cleveland. Frank Leslie's illustrated weekly, v. 76, Mar. 9, 1893: 154-155. AP2.L52, v. 76

Illustrations on p. 145, 149, 152-153, 156.

827

Bain, George G. Some snap-shots at the inauguration. Frank Leslie's illustrated weekly, v. 76, Mar. 16, 1893: 171. AP2.L52, v. 76

Illustrations on p. 168, 169.

828

Field, Kate. A worm's inaugural remarks; the inaugural procession. Kate Field's Washington, v. 7, Mar. 8, 1893: 145-146. AP2.K27, v. 7

829

Foote, Kate. Our Washington letter. Independent, v. 45, Mar. 9, 1893: 6-7. AP2.I53, v. 45

830

Inauguration ceremonies. Congressional record, 53d Congress, special session of the Senate, v. 25, Mar. 4, 1893: 2-4. J11.R5, v. 25

831

Inauguration of President Cleveland. Illustrated American, v. 13, Mar. 25, 1893: 359-365. illus. AP2.I25, v. 13

Another illustration on p. 358.

832

Inauguration of the President of the United States, March 4, 1893. Card of admission. [Washington] Bureau Engraving & Print. [1893] 1 p. illus. DWP

In Cleveland 1893 folder.

833
Lingle, Caroline G. Inauguration reminiscences. Kate Field's Washington, v. 7, Mar. 15, 1893: 166-167. AP2.K27, v. 7

834
Nelson, Henry L. The inauguration of President Cleveland. Harper's weekly, v. 37, Mar. 18, 1893: 251. AP2.H32, v. 37

Illustrations on p. 245, 252, 253, 256-257.

835
Proctor, John C. When the Democrats staged their most riotous inaugural. Sunday star (Washington), Aug. 26, 1951: C-2. Newsp

836
Smith, Percy G. Inauguration preparations; interesting details of the process of President-making. Kate Field's Washington, v. 7, Mar. 1, 1893: 133-134. AP2.K27, v. 7

837
U.S. *Congress. Senate. Committee of Arrangements for the Inauguration, 1893.* Order of procession for the inauguration of the President of the United States on the fourth of March, 1893. [Washington] Bureau Engraving & Print. [1893] [4] p. illus. Mss

In U.S. Miscellany, Executive Mansion.
Copy also in DWP, in Cleveland 1893 folder.

838
Washington, D.C. Headquarters of the Grand Marshal, *1893.* Inaugural parade of March 4, 1893. [Washington, 1893?] 16 p. (General orders, no. 1) F199.W31 1893G

839
Washington, D.C. Inaugural Committee, *1893.* Cleveland and Stevenson, inaugural ceremonies, March 4, 1893. Officers and members of the General, Executive, and Sub-committees. [Washington, 1893] 60 p. F199.W31 1893C

840
Washington, D.C. Inaugural Committee, *1893.* Inaugural ceremonies of Grover Cleveland, President, and Adlai E. Stevenson, Vice-President.

March 4, 1893. Final report of the General Committee and of the Executive Committee. [Washington, Printed by J. F. Sheiry, 1893] 48 p. illus. F199.W31 1893I

William McKinley

841

Banks, Elizabeth L. Sentiments of the inaugural crowd. Washington post, Mar. 7, 1897: 6. Newsp

842

Barbee, David R. Queen Lil attended M'Kinley inaugural; fair skies helped to make 1897 event one of most brilliant in Capital. *In* The Washington post. Inaugural edition, Saturday, March 4, 1933. Washington, 1933. p. 11. E806.W28

843

Davis, Richard Harding. The inauguration. Harper's monthly, v. 95, Aug. 1897: 337-355. illus. AP2.H3, v. 95

Reprinted, minus two illustrations, in his *A Year From a Reporter's Note-Book* (New York, Harper, 1898. D398.D3), p. 137-189.

844

Decorations for President McKinley's inauguration. American architect and building news, v. 55, Mar. 27, 1897: 100. NA1.A3, v. 55

845

Forbes, Quincy. At the Nation's Capital: the inauguration. Illustrated American, v. 21, Mar. 13, 1897: 360-362. illus. AP2.I25, v. 21

Another illustration on p. 359.

846

Gillam, Victor. The triumphal entry of McKinley, March 4th, 1897. Judge, v. 32, Mar. 13, 1897: 172-173. col. lithograph. 27.5 x 46 cm. AP101.J8, v. 32

Caricature of inaugural procession as a Roman triumph.

847

Inaugural day. Outlook, v. 55, Mar. 13, 1897: 722-723.
AP2.O8, v. 55

848

Inauguration ceremonies. Congressional record, 55th Congress, special session of the Senate, v. 30, Mar. 4, 1897: 2-5. J11.R5, v. 30

849

Inauguration, March 4, 1897. [Admission tickets to reviewing stand for President and Mrs. Grover Cleveland. Washington, 1897] Mss

Accompanied by form letter from chairman of Inaugural Committee. Ticket to inaugural ball indicated in letter as being enclosed is not now in envelope.

In U.S. Miscellany, Executive Mansion.

850

The inauguration of McKinley. Leslie's weekly, v. 84, Mar. 18, 1897: 173. AP2.L52, v. 84

Illustrations and captions only; no other text. Other illustrations on p. 180, 181.

851

Jennings, Janet. Our Washington letter. Independent, v. 49, Mar. 11, 1897: 9. AP2.I53, v. 49

852

Leech, Margaret. In the days of McKinley. New York, Harper [1959] 686 p. illus., facsims., ports. E711.6.L4

First inauguration: p. 116-120,
Second inauguration: p. 573-575.
T. Roosevelt's inauguration: p. 602.

853

Morgan, Howard Wayne. William McKinley and his America. [Syracuse, N.Y.] Syracuse University Press, 1963. 595 p. illus., ports. E711.6.M7

First inauguration: p. 272-273.
Second inauguration: p. 510-512.

854

Nelson, Henry L. The inauguration of Mr. McKinley. Harper's weekly, v. 41, Mar. 13, 1897: 259. AP2.H32, v. 41

Illustrations on p. 241, 248, 257, and 260-261.

President McKinley reviewing the inaugural procession from the stand in front of the White House. From *Harper's Weekly*—see item 854.

855

The Presidential inauguration in the United States. Illustrated London news, v. 110, Mar. 20, 1897: 389. illus. AP4.I3, v. 110

856

Souvenir program of the inaugural ceremonies of Wm. McKinley, President, and Garret A. Hobart, Vice-President of the United States, March 4, 1897. [Washington] Published by U.S. Historical and Souvenir Pub. Co. [1897] 36 p. illus. DWP

In McKinley folder.

857

U.S. *Congress. Senate. Committee of Arrangements for the Inauguration, 1897.* Program for the inauguration of the President and Vice-President of the United States, March fourth, 1897. [Washington, Govt. Print. Off. Print, 1897] [8] p. F199.U58

858

U.S. *President, 1897-1901 (McKinley)* Inaugural address of William McKinley, March 4, 1897. Washington, Govt. Print. Off., 1897. 12 p. J82.C81 Mar. 4

859

Washington, D.C. Inaugural Committee, *1897.* Inaugural ceremonies, March 4th, 1897. Final report of the chairman of the Executive Committee. Washington, Gibson Bros., 1897. 24 p. F199.W31 1897 In

860

Washington, D.C. Inaugural Committee, *1897.* Inaugural ceremonies, Washington, D.C., March 4th, 1897; souvenier [sic] of National Capitol. [Washington] 1897. 48 p. illus. F199.W31 1897I

861

Washington, D.C. Inaugural Committee, *1897.* Official programme of the inaugural ceremonies of Hon. William McKinley, of Ohio, and Hon. Garret A. Hobart, of New Jersey, as President and Vice-President of the United States, at Washington, D.C., March 4, 1897; edited and compiled by Robert Schenck Fletcher and Fred. W. Evans. [Washington?] Brett Lithographing Co., c1897. 96 p. illus. F199.W31 1897O

William McKinley
Second Inauguration

862

Batchelder, Frank R. Mrs. Damon's inauguration boarder. Leslie's weekly, v. 92, Mar. 2, 1901: 201. AP2.L52, v. 92

Short story.

863

Chapple, Joseph Mitchell. [The inauguration] National magazine, v. 14, Apr. 1901: 6, 8-17. illus. AP2.N34, v. 14

864

Fawcett, Waldon. The first inauguration of the new century. Leslie's weekly, v. 92, Mar. 2, 1901: 210-211. ports. AP2.L52, v. 92

Other illustrations on p. 212.

865

Gillam, Victor. The inauguration of William McKinley, March 4th, 1901. Judge, v. 40, Mar. 9, 1901. col. lithograph. 27 x 45.5 cm. AP101.J8, v. 40

Caricature of inaugural procession showing McKinley in sedan chair shaped like the "full dinner pail." Pages of volume are unnumbered.

866

A great occasion. Washington Capital, v. 20, Mar. 9, 1901: 3. F191.W27, v. 20

867

The inaugural ceremonies. Independent, v. 53, Mar. 7, 1901: 521. AP2.I53, v. 53

868

The inauguration. Outlook, v. 67, Mar. 9, 1901: 555. AP2.O8, v. 67

869

Inauguration ceremonies. Congressional record, 57th Congress, special session of the Senate, v. 35, Mar. 4, 1901: 2-3. J11.R5, v. 35

870

The inauguration of McKinley and Roosevelt. Leslie's weekly, v. 92, Mar. 16, 1901: 257. illus. AP2.L52, v. 92

This page was reprinted in v. 93, extra no., Sept. 9, 1901, p. [12].

871

Inauguration of the President of the United States, March fourth, nineteen hundred and one. [Admission ticket. Washington, 1901] 1 p. ports. Mss

In U.S. Miscellany, Executive Mansion.

872

Irving, Minna. His first inauguration day. Leslie's weekly, v. 92, Mar. 2, 1901: 211. AP2.L52, v. 92

Poem.

873

Irving, Minna. Inauguration day. Leslie's weekly, v. 92, Mar. 9, 1901: 223. AP2.L52, v. 92

Poem.

874

Leupp, Francis E. The inauguration. Harper's weekly, v. 45, Mar. 9, 1901: 246. AP2.H32, v. 45

Illustrations on p. 243, 248, 255, and 260-261.

875

Palmer, Frederick. The Presidential inauguration. Collier's weekly, v. 26, Mar. 16, 1901: 6-7, 13. illus. AP2.C65, v. 26

Other illustrations on p. 5, 8, and 16-17.

876

U.S. *Congress. Joint Committee of Arrangements for the Inauguration, 1901.* Program for the inauguration of the President and Vice-President of the United States, March 4th, 1901. [Washington, Govt. Print. Off., 1901] 10 p. ports. Mss

In U.S. Miscellany, Executive Mansion.

877

U.S. *President, 1897-1901 (McKinley)* Inaugural address of William McKinley, March 4, 1901. Washington, Govt. Print. Off., 1901. 31 p. J82.C85 Mch. 4

878

Washington, D.C. Headquarters of the Grand Marshal, *1901.* Inaugural parade of March 4, 1901. [Washington, Gibson Bros., 1901] 19 p. (General orders, no. 5) DWP

In McKinley folder.

879

Washington, D.C. Inaugural Committee, *1901.* Inaugural ceremonies, March 4, 1901. Committees in charge and rules for their government adopted by the Inaugural Committee, December 17, 1900. [Washington, National Pub. Co., 1901?] 52 p. DWP

In McKinley folder.

880

Washington, D.C. Inaugural Committee, *1901.* Official souvenir program, inaugural ceremonies, March 4, 1901. Edited and compiled by the Committee on Printing, Isadore Saks, chairman. [Washington, 1901] [104] p. illus. F199.W31 1901O

Theodore Roosevelt

881

The accession of President Roosevelt. Outlook, v. 69, Sept. 21, 1901: 144. AP2.O8, v. 69

882

The inauguration of Theodore Roosevelt. Harper's weekly, v. 45, Sept. 21, 1901: 957. AP2.H32, v. 45

883

Mowbray, Jay H. The intellectual giant, Roosevelt, the people's champion for human rights. Philadelphia, National Pub. Co. [c1912] 128, 64, [160] p. illus., plates (part col.) JK2388.1912.M7

First inauguration of Theodore Roosevelt: p. [100]-[103].

884

The new President takes the oath of office. Leslie's weekly, v. 93, Sept. 28, 1901: 293. illus. AP2.L52, v. 93

Pictures show the house and room where President Roosevelt was sworn in.

885

Pringle, Henry F. Theodore Roosevelt, a biography. New York, Harcourt, Brace [c1931] 627 p. plates, ports. E757.P96

First inauguration: p. 232-233.

Second inauguration: p. 362-365.

A revised edition of 1956 (New York, Harcourt, Brace. 435 p. A Harvest book, 15. E757.P967), somewhat abridged, gives substantially the same information on p. 163-164 and p. 255-257.

886

[Theodore Roosevelt is sworn in as President]. National magazine, v. 15, Oct. 1901: 22, 24. AP2.N34, v. 15

Theodore Roosevelt
Second Inauguration

887

Baker Abby G. Inauguration day at the National Capital. Woman's home companion, v. 32, Mar. 1905: 52. AP2.W714, v. 32

888

Barbee, David R. Cowboys featured Roosevelt parade; Rough Riders also in long march of the inaugural; cheered by crowds. *In* The Washington post. Inaugural edition, Saturday, March 4, 1933. Washington, 1933. p. 3. E806.W28

889

Blythe, Samuel G. A President is inaugurated. *In* Greene, Ward, *ed.* Star reporters and 34 of their stories. New York, Random House [1948] p. 71-77. PN4726.G7 1948

First published in the *New York World* on Mar. 5, 1905.

890

Chapple, Joseph Mitchell. [The inauguration]. National magazine, v. 22, Apr. 1905: 3-6. illus. AP2.N34, v. 22

891

District of Columbia. *Board of Commissioners.* Inaugural laws, to be enforced by the police, February 28th to March 10th, inclusive, in the District of Columbia. [Washington] Press of Judd & Detweiler [1905] broadside. 49 x 31 cm. DWP

In Theodore Roosevelt folder.

892

Finest inaugural parade ever held in Washington; imposing inauguration of President Roosevelt. Leslie's weekly, v. 100, Mar. 16, 1905: 244-245. AP2.L52, v. 100

Illustrations and captions only; no other text.

893

Friggens, Paul G. Teddy's inaugural recalled out West; reminiscences of the trip to Washington made by sixty-two cowboys to take part in that historic inaugural parade of twenty-eight years ago. Sunday star (Washington), Mar. 5, 1933, pt. 7: 41. illus. Newsp

894

Hapgood, Norman. Washington's inaugural, and Mr. Roosevelt's; a glance from 1789 to 1905—our country then and now. Collier's, v. 34, Mar. 4, 1905: 17. AP2.C65, v. 34

895

Hitchcock, F. H. The inauguration. Harper's weekly. v, 49, Mar. 4, 1905: 304-306. illus. AP2.H32, v. 49

Another illustration on p. 299.

896

[The inauguration]. Outlook, v. 79, Mar. 11, 1905: 626-628. AP2.O8, v. 79

897

[Inauguration ceremonies]. Congressional record, 59th Congress, special session of the Senate, v. 40, Mar. 4, 1905: 2-3. J11.R5, v. 40

898

Inauguration ceremonies, March fourth, 1905. [Admission ticket to platform outside Senate wing of Capitol. Washington, 1905] 1 p. DWP

Accompanied by informative note.
In Theodore Roosevelt folder.

899

Inauguration of President Roosevelt. Independent, v. 58, Mar. 9, 1905: 517-519. illus. AP2.I53, v. 58

900
Irving, Minna. Inauguration–President Roosevelt, March 4th, 1905. Leslie's weekly, v. 100, Mar. 2, 1905: 210. AP2.L52, v. 100

Poem.

901
Keppler, Joseph. Ave Theodore! Puck, v. 57, Mar. 1, 1905. col. lithograph. 26.5 x 44.8 cm. AP101.P7, v. 57

Caricature of inaugural procession as a Roman triumph. Pages of volume are unnumbered.

902
Official programme of exercises and illustrated inaugural history commemorating the inauguration of Theodore Roosevelt as President of the United States, Charles W. Fairbanks as Vice-President of the United States; illustrated with more than one hundred and fifty engravings. Washington, O. A. Sontag, 1905. 108 p. illus.
JK538.1905.O3

903
Precedent set when T. R. wins office in own right. Washington herald, Mar. 4, 1933: 11-B. Newsp

904
The President and inauguration-day ceremonies in Washington. Harper's weekly, v. 49, Mar. 18, 1905: 394-395. illus. AP2.H32, v. 49

905
Roosevelt, Theodore, *Pres. U.S.* Letters, selected and edited by Elting E. Morison. v. 4. The Square Deal, 1903-1905. Cambridge, Harvard University Press, 1951. 711-1438 p. E757.R7958, v. 4

Inauguration: p. 1131-1133.

906
Souvenir programme of the inaugural of Theodore Roosevelt, March 4, 1905. [Washington, 1905?] [41] p. illus. F199.W3137

907
Thaw, Alexander B. An inaugural ode. Nelson, N.H., Monadnock Press, 1905. 20 p. PS3539.H1515 1905

908

U.S. *Congress. Joint Committee of Arrangements for the Inauguration, 1905.* Program, inauguration of the President and Vice-President of the United States. Ceremonies at the National Capitol, March fourth, nineteen hundred and five. [Washington, Govt. Print. Off., 1905] 8 p. illus. DWP

In Theodore Roosevelt folder.

909

Washington, D.C. Inaugural Committee, *1905.* Final report of the chairman of the Inaugural Committee and of the chairmen of the several sub-committees in connection with the inaugural ceremonies of March 4, 1905. Washington, W. F. Roberts Co. [1905] 119 p. F199.W31 1905F

910

Washington, D.C. Inaugural Committee, *1905.* The following organizations will compose the civic grand division of the inaugural parade, 1905. [Washington, 1905] [4] p. MiU-C

911

Washington, D.C. Inaugural Committee, *1905.* Inaugural parade of March 4, 1905. Headquarters civic grand division. General order no. 2, Washington, March 2, 1905. [Washington, 1905] 2 l. MiU-C

912

Washington, D.C. Inaugural Committee, *1905.* Inaugural souvenir, 1905. [Washington, Press of W. F. Roberts Co., 1905] [24] p. F199.W31 1905In

Copy also in DWP, in Theodore Roosevelt folder.

913

Washington, D.C. Inaugural Committee, *1905.* Inauguration of Theodore Roosevelt as President of the United States, March 4, 1905; membership and duties of committees in charge of inaugural ceremonies. Washington, Headquarters of the Inaugural Committee [1905] 48 p. F199.W31 1905I

William Howard Taft

914

Barbee, David R. Blizzard spoiled Taft inauguration; awful weather caused oath to be administered in Senate chamber. *In* The Washington post. Inaugural edition, Saturday, March 4, 1933. Washington, 1933. p. 18. E806.W28

915

Chapple, Joseph Mitchell. Affairs at Washington. National magazine, v. 30, Apr. 1909: 1-4. illus. AP2.N34, v. 30

Page numbering is irregular; there are actually 9 p. of text and illustrations.

916

Cobb, Irvin S. The hotel clerk expands on the inauguration. Sunday star (Washington), Feb. 28, 1909, pt. 4: 5. illus. Newsp

917

Humors of inauguration. Washington post, Mar. 7, 1909, magazine section: 10. illus. Newsp

918

Inaugural address. Congressional record, 61st Congress, special session of the Senate, v. 44, Mar. 4, 1909: 2-5. J11.R5, v. 44

919

[The inauguration]. Current literature, v. 46, Apr. 1909: 347-349. AP2.C95, v. 46

Illustrations on p. 350-356.

920

The inauguration. Outlook, v. 91, Mar. 13, 1909: 565-566. AP2.O8, v. 91

921

[The inauguration]. Outlook, v. 91, Mar. 13, 1909: 580-583. AP2.O8, v. 91

922

The inauguration of President Taft. Harper's weekly, v. 53, Mar. 13, 1909: 4. AP2.H32, v. 53

Illustrations on p. 3, 8, 9, 18-19; cartoons on p. 32. A note on the ball appears on p. 5-6.

325-882 O-69—10

923

Inauguration of President Taft. Independent, v. 66, Mar. 11, 1909: 503-504. AP2.I53, v. 66

Illustration on p. 505.

924

[Invitation to] the ceremonies attending the inauguration of the President of the United States, March fourth, nineteen hundred and nine. [Washington, 1909] folder. DWP

Text on p. [1]. Two portraits laid in.
Two copies in Taft folder.

925

The last "stir" of the Roosevelt administration: Mr. Taft inaugurated in a blizzard at Washington. Illustrated London news, v. 134, Mar. 20, 1909: 428. illus. AP4.I3, v. 150

See also caption to portrait in issue of Mar. 6, 1909, p. 333.

926

Leonard, William Ellery. Inauguration ode, March 4, 1909. La Follette's weekly magazine, v. 1, Mar. 6, 1909: 9. AP2.L28, v. 1

927

Lewis, Judd M. The inauguration. Collier's, v. 42, Mar. 6, 1909: 20. AP2.C65, v. 42

Poem.

928

McHale, Francis. Inauguration as President. *In his* President and Chief Justice; the life and public services of William Howard Taft. Philadelphia, Dorrance [c1931] p. 157-163. E762.M22

929

Pringle, Henry F. The life and times of William Howard Taft, a biography. New York, Farrar & Rinehart [c1939] 2 v. (1106 p.) facsims., plates, ports. E762.P75

Inauguration: v. 1, p. 393-398.
Wilson's first inauguration: v. 2, p. 854-855.

930

Ross, Ishbel. An American family; the Tafts, 1678 to 1964. Cleveland, World Pub. Co. [1964] 468 p. illus. E762.R6

Inauguration and inaugural ball: p. 209-212.

931

Taft, Helen (Herron). Recollections of full years; what it is like to enter the White House as First Lady of the land. Delineator, v. 84, May 1914: 5-6, 66-68. illus. TT500.D3, v. 84

Also published in her *Recollections of Full Years* (New York, Dodd, Mead, 1914. E762.1.T12), p. 325-333.

932

Taft inaugural held indoors. Washington herald, Mar. 4, 1933: 11-B. Newsp

933

Taft was blithe in 10-inch snow. Washington post, Jan. 20, 1961: A-11. Newsp

934

Unique features of the Taft inauguration. Washington post, Mar. 5, 1909: 18. Newsp

935

U.S. *Congress. Joint Committee of Arrangements for the Inauguration, 1909.* Program of the ceremonies attending the inauguration of the President and Vice-President of the United States at the National Capitol, March fourth, nineteen hundred and nine. Washington, 1909. [8] l. DWP

Two copies in Taft folder.

936

U.S. *President, 1909-1913 (Taft)* Inaugural address of President Taft, March 4, 1909. Washington, Govt. Print. Off., 1909. 15 p. J82.D11 Mch. 4

937

U.S. *President, 1909-1913 (Taft)* Inaugural address of President Taft, March 4, 1909. Washington, Govt. Print. Off., 1909. 68 p. J82.D11 March 4a Rare Bk. Coll.

938

Washington, D.C. Inaugural Committee, *1909.* Final reports of chairmen of committees to Edward J. Stellwagen, chairman of the committee in charge of the inauguration of William Howard Taft as President of the United States and James Schoolcraft Sherman as Vice-President of the United States at Washington, D.C., March 4, 1909. [Washington, Press of W. F. Roberts Co., 1909?] 189 p. illus. JK538.1909.W3

939

Washington, D.C. Inaugural Committee, *1909.* Inauguration ceremonies, March 4, 1909. Inaugural souvenir, 1909. [Washington, Press of W. F. Roberts Co., c1909] [12] p. plates, ports. E761.W3

Two copies also in DWP, Taft folder.

940

Washington, D.C. Inaugural Committee, *1909.* Inauguration of William Howard Taft, as President of the United States, and James Schoolcraft Sherman, as Vice-President of the United States, March 4, 1909, Washington, D.C.: membership and duties of committees. [Washington, Press of W. F. Roberts Co., 1909] 59 p. F199.W31 1909I

941

Washington, D.C. Inaugural Committee, *1909.* Official program, inauguration ceremonies, March 4, 1909. [Washington, G. E. Howard Press, 1909] 32 p. illus. F199.W31 1909O

942

Watkins, John E. Unique features of inauguration of William H. Taft. Sunday star (Washington), Feb. 21, 1909, pt. 4: 5. illus. Newsp

943

Weir, Hugh C. Inaugurating a President in a blizzard. World today, v. 16, Apr. 1909: 359-362. illus. AP2.H4, v. 16

Woodrow Wilson

944

Adams, Franklin P. An ode in time of inauguration. Collier's, v. 50, Mar. 8, 1913: 23-24. AP2.C65, v. 50

945

Baker, Ray Stannard. Woodrow Wilson; life and letters. Garden City, N.Y., Doubleday, Page, 1927-39. 8 v. facsims., plates, ports.

E767.B16

First inauguration: v. 4, p. 1-11.
Second inauguration: v. 6, p. 482-483.

946

Barbee, David R. Wilson inaugural most spectacular; Princeton and South joined in joyous welcome to Jersey Governor. *In* The Washington post. Inaugural edition, Saturday, March 4, 1933. Washington, 1933. p. 2. E806.W28

947

The ceremonies. Outlook, v. 103, Mar. 15, 1913: 553-554.

AP2.O8, v. 103

948

Ceremonies incident to the inauguration of Woodrow Wilson as President and Thomas R. Marshall as Vice-President of the United States. Washington at a glance. [Washington, Southern Railway, 1913?] 40 p. illus. (part col.), map, ports. DWP

In Wilson 1913 folder.

949

Chapple, Joseph Mitchell. The inauguration of President Wilson. National magazine, v. 38, Apr. 1913: 17-28. illus. AP2.N34, v. 38

Additional comments by Chapple on the inauguration appear on p. 1-3.

950

Considine, Robert B. On the line: the avenue sanded for horses during the Wilson inauguration. Times-herald (Washington), Jan. 19, 1949: 15.

Newsp

Includes recollections of some other inaugurations.

951

Eaton, William D., *and* Harry C. Read. Woodrow Wilson, his life and work. [Chicago, Printed by Peterson Co.] 1919. 769 p. illus. (part col.), map, plan. E767.E14

First inauguration and address: p. 75-82.
Second inaugural address: p. 404-409.

952

Fouquières, André de. A French author's impressions of the inauguration. New York times, Mar. 9, 1913, pt. 7: 11. illus. Newsp

953

Hoover, Irwin H. Taft out–Wilson in: a typical inauguration day. *In his* Forty-two years in the White House. Boston, Houghton Mifflin Co., 1934. p. [49]-59. plates, ports. E176. 1.H78

954

[Inauguration of the President of the United States]. Congressional record, 63d Congress, special session of the Senate, v. 50, Mar. 4, 1913: 2-3. J11.R5, v. 50

955

[Invitation to] the ceremonies attending the inauguration of the President of the United States, March fourth, nineteen hundred and thirteen. [Washington, 1913] 1 p. DWP

Accompanied by 2 portraits.
In Wilson 1913 folder.

956

Irwin, Wallace. Inavgvralia; a timely miracle play. Collier's, v. 50, Mar. 8, 1913: 17, 29. AP2.C65, v. 50

957

Link, Arthur S. Wilson. [v. 2] The new freedom. Princeton, N.J., Princeton University Press, 1956. 504 p. illus. E767.L65, v. 2

First inauguration: p. 57-60.

958

Lord, Frank B. The inauguration. National monthly, v. 4, Mar. 1913: 237-238, 248-250. illus. AP2.N348, v. 4

959

Mason, Walt. Inauguration day. Collier's, v. 50, Mar. 8, 1913: 24. AP2.C65, v. 50

Poem.

960
The Nation greets the new administration. Leslie's illustrated weekly newspaper, v. 116, Mar. 13, 1913: 268-269. AP2.L52, v. 116

Illustrations and captions only; no other text.

961
Ruhl, Arthur. At the inauguration. Collier's, v. 51, Mar. 22, 1913: 15, 29-30. illus. AP2.C65, v. 51

962
Smith, Gene. When the cheering stopped; the last years of Woodrow Wilson. With an introduction by Allan Nevins. New York, W. Morrow, 1964. 307 p. illus., ports. E767.S65

Wilson's first inauguration: p. 4-5.
Harding's inauguration: p. 183-186.

963
Special missions welcome President Wilson. *In* Pan American Union. Bulletin, v. 36, Mar. 1913: 415-427. illus., ports. F1403.B955, v. 36

964
Tumulty, Joseph P. Woodrow Wilson as I know him. Garden City, N.Y., Doubleday, Page, 1921. 553 p. facsims., ports. E767.T9

First inauguration: p. 139-143.
Harding's inauguration: p. 506-511.

965
U.S. *Congress. Joint Committee of Arrangements for the Inauguration, 1913.* Program of the ceremonies attending the inauguration of the President and Vice President of the United States at the National Capitol, March fourth, nineteen hundred thirteen. [Washington, 1913] [8] l. DWP

In Wilson 1913 folder.

966
U.S. *President, 1913-1921 (Wilson)* Inaugural address of President Wilson, delivered at the Capitol, March 4, 1913. [New York] Priv. print. [Scribner Press] 1913. 10 p. J82.D21 Mch 4a

967

U.S. *President, 1913-1921 (Wilson)* Inaugural address of President Wilson, delivered at the Capitol, March 4, 1913. Washington [Govt. Print. Off.] 1913. 8 p. J82.D21 Mch 4

968

U.S. *President, 1913-1921 (Wilson)* Inaugural addresses of President Woodrow Wilson and Vice President Thomas R. Marshall, delivered before the Senate of the United States March 4, 1913. Washington, Govt. Print. Off., 1913. 9 p. ([U.S.] 63d Congress, speical session. Senate document 3) J82.D21 Mch 4d

969

[Views of the inauguration]. National monthly, v. 4, Apr. 1913: 261, 268-269. illus. AP2.N348, v. 4

Brief captions only; no text. Another illustration on cover.

970

Walworth, Arthur C. Woodrow Wilson. 2d ed., rev. Boston, Houghton Mifflin Co., 1965. xiv, 436, 439 p. port. E767.W34 1965

First inauguration: pt. 1, p. 262-266.
Second inauguration: pt. 2, p. 91-92.
Harding's inauguration: pt. 2, p. 408-409.

971

Washington, D.C. Inaugural Committee, *1913.* Final reports of chairmen of committees to William Corcoran Eustis, chairman of the committee in charge of the inauguration of Woodrow Wilson ... and Thomas R. Marshall. Washington, 1913. RPB

972

Washington, D.C. Inaugural Committee, *1913.* Official program, inauguration ceremonies, March fourth, 1913. [Washington, Printed by Judd & Detweiler] c1913. [27] p. F199.W31 1913

Woodrow Wilson
Second Inauguration

973

The inauguration. Outlook, v. 115, Mar. 14, 1917: 448. AP2.O8, v. 115

974

Inauguration of the President of the United States. Congressional record, 65th Congress, special session of the Senate, v. 55, Mar. 5, 1917: 2-3. J11.R5, v. 55

975

[Invitation to] the inauguration of the President of the United States, March fifth, nineteen hundred and seventeen. [Washington, 1917] folder. DWP

Text on p. [1]. Two portraits laid in.
In Wilson 1917 folder.

976

Link, Arthur S. Wilson. [v. 5] Campaigns for progressivism and peace, 1916-1917. Princeton, N.J., Princeton University Press, 1956. 464 p. illus. E767.L65, v. 5

Second inauguration: p. 367-369.

977

President Wilson's inaugural [text]. Independent, v. 89, Mar. 12, 1917: 432. AP2.I53, v. 89

Several illustrations appear in the issue of Mar. 19, p. 491.

978

[President Wilson's inauguration]. Illustrated London news, v. 150, Apr. 14, 1917: 425. illus. AP4.I3, v. 150

979

U.S. *Congress. Joint Committee on Arrangements for the Inauguration, 1917.* Program of the ceremonies attending the inauguration of the President and Vice President of the United States at the National Capitol, March fifth, nineteen hundred and seventeen. [Washington, 1917] [11] l. DWP

Two copies in Wilson 1917 folder.

980

U.S. *President, 1913-1921 (Wilson)* Inaugural address of President Woodrow Wilson. Address of the President of the United States, delivered at the inaugural exercises held on March 5, 1917. Washington, Govt. Print. Off., 1917. 6 p. ([U.S.] 65th Congress, special session. Senate document 2) J82.D25 Mar. 5

981

Washington, D.C. Inaugural Committee, *1917.* The official souvenir program, second inauguration, Woodrow Wilson, President, Thomas R. Marshall, Vice President, of the United States, the fifth of March, nineteen-seventeen. [Washington, Thomsen-Bryan-Ellis Co., 1917] [32] p. illus., ports. DLC

Two copies also in DWP, in Wilson 1917 folder.

982

Washington, D.C. Inaugural Committee, *1917.* Second inauguration of Woodrow Wilson as President of the United States and Thomas Riley Marshall as Vice President of the United States. March 5, 1917. Washington, Govt. Print. Off., 1918. 167 p. illus. ([U.S.] 65th Congress, 1st session. Senate document 116) F199.W31 1917

983

Wilson, Edith (Bolling) Galt. My memoir. Indianapolis, Bobbs-Merrill Co. [c1939] 386 p. facsims., plates, ports. E767.3.W55

Second inauguration: p. 130.
Harding's inauguration: p. 317-319.

984

Wilson again our President. Leslie's illustrated weekly newspaper, v. 124, Mar. 15, 1917: 294. illus. AP2.L52, v. 124

Warren G. Harding

985

Adams, Samuel H. Incredible era; the life and times of Warren Gamaliel Harding. Boston, Houghton Mifflin Co., 1939. 456 p. plates, ports. E786.A34

Inauguration: p. 209-211.

986

Amplifier for Harding's address has successful try-out at plaza. Sunday star (Washington), Feb. 27, 1921, pt. 1: 14. Newsp

987

Back to Jefferson. Independent, v. 105, Jan. 22, 1921: 91. AP2.I53, v. 105

988

Baldwin, Elbert F. Exit Wilson; enter Harding. Outlook, v. 127, Mar. 16, 1921: 414-415. illus. AP2.O8, v. 127

Other illustrations on p. 413.

989

Chapple, Joseph Mitchell. A simple inauguration ceremony as Harding wished. *In his* Life and times of Warren G. Harding, our after-war President. Boston, Chapple Pub. Co., 1924. p. 159-168. illus. E786.C45

990

Du Puy, William A. When Harding told Wilson the story of an elephant. What do Presidents talk about during ride down the avenue? War President heard tale of beast that loved his keeper. Washington daily news, Mar. 4, 1933: 24. Newsp

991

The Harding inauguration. National magazine, v. 50, Apr. 1921: 18-20. illus. AP2.N34, v. 50

992

[The inauguration of President Harding]. Illustrated London news, v. 158, Mar. 26, 1921: 415. illus. AP4.I3, v. 158

993

Inauguration of the President of the United States. Congressional record, 67th Congress, special session of the Senate, v. 61, Mar. 4, 1921: 4-6. J11.R5, v. 61

994

Lardner, Ring W. "Dressing for inauguration is some job," says Lardner. Sunday star (Washington), Feb. 27, 1921, pt. 4: 2. illus. Newsp

995

Lardner, Ring W. "Well, the visiters is all here to see the simple ceremonys." Evening star (Washington), Mar. 3, 1921: 1-2. Newsp

996

Lardner, Ring W. "What's inauguration if Harding can't wear his silver plaque?" Evening star (Washington), Mar. 4, 1921: 9. Newsp

997

President Harding's inauguration. Current history, v. 14, Apr. 1921: 39-44. illus. D410.C8, v. 14

Another illustration on p. 1.

998

The Rambler: what sort of day was March 4, 1921. Evening star (Washington), Mar. 4, 1957: B-1. Newsp

999

Russell, Thomas H. Inauguration day. *In his* The illustrious life and work of Warren G. Harding, twenty-ninth President of the United States. [Chicago, 1923] p. 99-116. illus. E786.R96

1000

Shackleton, Robert. An inauguration. *In his* The book of Washington. Philadelphia, Penn Pub. Co., 1922. p. 357-367. illus. F199.S49

1001

Sinclair, Andrew. The available man; the life behind the masks of Warren Gamaliel Harding. New York, Macmillan [1965] 344 p. illus., ports. E786.S5

Inauguration and address: p. 198-199.

1002

"A telephone achievement ranking with the opening of the transcontinental line." Transmitter, v. 9, Mar. 1921: 1-6. illus. TK1.T7, v. 9

Bell public address system makes it possible for Harding's inaugural address to be heard by everyone assembled at the scene.

1003

U.S. *President, 1921-1923 (Harding)* Inaugural address of Hon. Warren G. Harding, President of the United States, March 4, 1921. Washington [Govt. Print. Off.] 1921. 13 p. J82.D31 Mch. 4

1004

U.S. *President, 1921-1923 (Harding)* Inaugural addresses of President Warren G. Harding and Vice President Calvin Coolidge delivered before the Senate of the United States on March 4, 1921. Washington, Govt. Print. Off., 1921. 12 p. ([U.S.] 67th Congress, special session of the Senate. Senate document 1) J82.D31 Mch. 4a

1005

Washington, D.C. Inaugural Committee, *1921. Committee on Illumination.* Papers, 1920-21. DWP

Includes correspondence, list of members, minutes, and scrapbook of clippings and pictures.

In Harding folder.

Calvin Coolidge

1006

Coolidge, Calvin, *Pres. U.S.* Calvin Coolidge takes the oath of office. *In* Commager, Henry S., *and* Allan Nevins, *eds.* The heritage of America. Rev. and enl. ed. Boston, Little, Brown, 1949. p. 1102-1104. E178.C7274

From his *Autobiography* (New York, Cosmopolitan Book Corp., 1929. E792.C6), p. 173-177.

1007

Coolidge takes the helm. Current opinion, v. 75, Sept. 1923: 265. AP2.C95, v. 75

1008

Fountain, Joe H. Homestead inaugural, being an eye-witness account of the administration of the Presidential oath of office to Calvin Coolidge in his father's homestead at Plymouth, Vermont, August 3, 1923. [St. Albans? Vt., 1950] [28] p. illus., port. E792.F67

1009

Fuess, Claude M. Calvin Coolidge, the man from Vermont. Boston, Little, Brown, 1940. 522 p. facsims., plates, ports. E792.F85

First inauguration: p. 308-311.

Second inauguration: p. 360-362.

1010

Lang, Louis J. How Coolidge got the news. Outlook, v. 135, Sept. 5, 1923: 22-25. illus. AP2.O8, v. 135

1011

McCoy, Donald R. Calvin Coolidge; the quiet President. New York, Macmillan [1967] 472 p. illus. E792.M117

First inauguration: p. 148-149.
Second inauguration: p. 264-266.
Hoover's inauguration: p. 395.

1012

The midnight oath. Ladies' home journal, v. 41, Apr. 1924: 17, 236. illus. AP2.L135, v. 41

Colored illustration on p. 16.

1013

Orton, Vrest. Calvin Coolidge's unique Vermont inauguration; the facts winnowed from the chaff: the authentic account of the swearing in of Calvin Coolidge as 30th President of the United States by his father at the Coolidge Homestead, Plymouth Notch, Vermont, in 1923. Rutland, Vt., Tuttle Pub. Co. [1960] 93 p. illus. E792.O7

1014

Ross, Ishbel. Grace Coolidge and her era; the story of a President's wife. New York, Dodd, Mead, 1962. 370 p. illus. E792.1.C6R6

Harding's inauguration: p. 60-61.
Swearing in of Coolidge: p. 77-81.
Coolidge's inauguration, 1925: p. 141-142.
Hoover's inauguration: p. 255.

1015

White, William Allen. A Puritan in Babylon, the story of Calvin Coolidge. New York, Macmillan Co., 1938. xvi, 460 p. port. E792.W577

First inauguration: p. 242-253.
Second inauguration: p. 314-316.
Hoover's inauguration: p. 419.

1016

Wilson, Charles M. Lamplight inauguration. American heritage, v. 15, Dec. 1963: 80-86. illus. E171.A43, v. 15

Calvin Coolidge
Second Inauguration

1017

Chapple, Joseph Mitchell. [The inauguration] National magazine, v. 53, Mar. 1925: 339-340. illus. AP2.N34, v. 53

1018

The day of days. Vox Presidentis. Time, v. 5, Mar. 16, 1925: 1-5. ports. AP2.T37, v. 5

Includes excerpts from the inaugural address.

1019

Evert, Lawrence. Inaugural scenes and ceremonies sent to all the Nation. Transmitter, v. 13, Apr. 1925: 8-12. illus. TK1.T7, v. 13

First radio transmission of inaugural ceremonies.

1020

Hoover, Irwin H. An inauguration that fell flat. *In his* Forty-two years in the White House. Boston, Houghton Mifflin Co., 1934. p. [139]-150. plates, ports. E176.1.H78

1021

Inauguration of the President of the United States. Congressional record, 69th Congress, special session of the Senate, v. 67, Mar. 4, 1925: 4-7. J11.R5, v. 67

1022

Keyes, Frances Parkinson (Wheeler). A story of friendly flags; an account of the festivities, grave and gay, attending the inauguration of President Coolidge. Good housekeeping, v. 80, May 1925: 30-31, 164, 167-168, 171-172, 174, 177-178, 181. ports. TX1.G7, v. 80

1023

Levy, Newman. Inauguration ode. Saturday evening post, v. 197, Jan. 3, 1925: 8. AP2.S2, v. 197

1024

Merritt, Dixon. The sacrifical oath. Outlook, v. 139, Mar. 18, 1925: 407-409. illus. AP2.O8, v. 139

1025

Mr. Coolidge inaugurated as elected President of the United States. Illustrated London news, v. 168, Mar. 21, 1925: 472. illus. AP4.I3, v. 168

Another illustration on p. 471.

1026

The plain inauguration. Commonweal, v. 1, Feb. 25, 1925: 421-422.
AP2.C6897, v. 1

1027

Sending pictures by wire and radio. National magazine, v. 53, Mar. 1925: 369-370. illus. AP2.N53, v. 53

Mainly about the use of phototelegraphy to send pictures of President Coolidge's inauguration.

1028

Thaw, Alexander B. March fourth, 1925. Evening star (Washington), Mar. 4, 1925: 2. Newsp

"... a revision of a poem written by the same author ... on the occasion of Theodore Roosevelt's inauguration in 1905."

1029

U.S. *President, 1923-1929 (Coolidge)* Inaugural address of the President of the United States. March 4, 1925. Washington, Govt. Print. Off., 1925. 9 p. J82.D43 Mar. 4

1030

Visualizing the inauguration in San Francisco. Transmitter, v. 13, Apr. 1925: 13-15. illus. TK1.T7, v. 13

First transmission of inaugural photographs by telephone wire.

1031

Walker, Helen. Miss Nobody at the inauguration. Commonweal, v. 1, Mar. 18, 1925: 515-517. AP2.C6897, v. 1

Herbert C. Hoover

1032

Chapple, Joseph Mitchell. Affairs at Washington. National magazine, v. 57, Mar. 1929: 243-248. illus. AP2.N34, v. 57

Other illustrations on cover of issue and on p. 242.

1033

The Chief. "My countrymen." Time, v. 13, Mar. 11, 1929: 9-10.
AP2.T37, v. 13

Includes excerpts from the inaugural address.

1034

Citizens' Joint Committee on National Representation for the District of Columbia. A souvenir of the inauguration of a President of the United States from whose election half-a-million American citizens were barred by constitutional disfranchisement. [Washington, 1929] folder (8 p.) illus. DWP

In Hoover folder.

1035

Davidson, Robert H. Inaugurating the President. Transmitter, v. 17, Apr. 1929: 3-8. illus. TK1.T7, v. 17

1036

District of Columbia. *Board of Commissioners.* Special regulations, inaugural period, 1929. Effective from February 25 to March 11, 1929, both dates inclusive, except as otherwise provided. Washington, U.S. Govt. Print. Off., 1929. 10 p. HE372.W3 1929

1037

District of Columbia. *Police Dept.* Inauguration, March 4, 1929. Washington, U.S. Govt. Print. Off., 1929. 14 p. (General orders no. 10) DWP

Copies in Hoover folder and in Hoover inauguration scrapbook.

1038

Dunn, Charles. Inaugural visitors; cartoons. Washingtonian, Mar. 1929: 14-15. illus. F191.W39, 1929

1039

Edgerton, Joseph S. Trying obstacles are faced in staging airplane parade; impressions of men who took part in inaugural air pageant are given by participant. Evening star (Washington), Mar. 5, 1929: 5. Newsp

1040

Gann, Dolly (Curtis). Inauguration day. *In her* Dolly Gann's book. Garden City, N.Y., Doubleday, Doran, 1933. p. 101-110. E748.G19G2

1041

Grunewald, Hudson. Bringing the world to Washington for inauguration via radio. Sunday star (Washington), Mar. 3, 1929, pt. 7: 1, 5. illus. Newsp

325-882 O-69—11

1042

Hoover, Herbert C., *Pres. U.S.* Memoirs. v. 2. The Cabinet and the Presidency, 1920-1933. New York, Macmillan, 1952. 405 p. illus., ports. E802.H7, v. 2

Inauguration: p. 222.

1043

[The inaugural ceremonies]. Illustrated London news, v. 174, Mar. 23, 1929: 492. illus. AP4.I3, v. 174

1044

Inauguration of the President. Congressional record, 71st Congress, special session of the Senate, v. 71, Mar. 4, 1929: 4-7. J11.R5, v. 71

1045

Lyons, Eugene. Herbert Hoover, a biography. Garden City, N.Y., Doubleday, 1964. 444 p. E802.L82

Inauguration: p. 183.
First inauguration of F. D. Roosevelt: p. 320-321.

1046

McGee, Dorothy H. Herbert Hoover: engineer, humanitarian, statesman. New York, Dodd, Mead, 1959. 307 p. illus. E802.M2

Inauguration: p. 222-223.

1047

Roberts, Chalmers M. 1929 inauguration recalled: all seemed sunny in spite of fog on day Hoover became President. Washington post, Oct. 21, 1964: A-3. Newsp

1048

U.S. *Congress. Joint Committee on Arrangements for the Inauguration, 1929.* Program of the ceremonies attending the inauguration of the President and Vice President of the United States at the National Capitol, March fourth, nineteen hundred twenty-nine. Washington, U.S. Govt. Print. Off., 1929. [12] l. illus. DWP

In Hoover folder.

1049

U.S. *President, 1929-1933 (Hoover)* Inaugural address of Herbert Hoover, President of the United States, delivered at the Capitol, Washington, D.C. March 4, 1929. Washington, U.S. Govt. Print. Off., 1929. 11 p. ([U.S.] 71st Congress. Special session. Senate document 1)
J82.D51 Mar 4

1050

U.S. *President, 1929-1933 (Hoover)* Inaugural address of Herbert Hoover, President of the United States, delivered at the National Capitol, Washington, D.C., Monday, March 4, 1929. [n.p., 1929?] 11 p.
J82.D51 Mar 4a

1051

Warren, Harris G. Herbert Hoover and the great depression. New York, Oxford University Press, 1959. 372 p. E801.W28

Inauguration: p. 51-53.
First inauguration of F. D. Roosevelt: p. 293-294.

1052

Washington, D.C. Headquarters of the Grand Marshal, *1929.* Escort for the President and Vice President. Washington, 1929. 4 l. (General orders, no. 4) DWP

In Hoover inauguration scrapbook.

1053

Washington, D.C. Headquarters of the Grand Marshal, *1929.* General orders. no. 1-3. Washington, 1928-29. 3 no. DWP

In Hoover folder.

1054

Washington, D.C. Inaugural Committee, *1929.* Official program of the inaugural ceremonies inducting into office Herbert Hoover, President of the United States, and Charles Curtis, Vice-President of the United States. Washington, 1929. [36] p. illus. F199.W31 1929O

1055

Washington, D.C. Inaugural Committee, *1929.* Report of Inaugural Committee for the inauguration of Herbert Hoover as President, Charles Curtis, as Vice-President, March 4, 1929. Washington, Crane Printing Co. [1929?] 143 p. illus. F199.W31 1929R

Franklin D. Roosevelt

1056

Adams, Frederick B. Mr. Roosevelt continues, as President and author. *In* Bibliographical Society of America. Papers, v. 37, 3d quarter, 1943: 223-232. Z1008.B51P, v. 37

Notes on editions of his first inaugural address.

1057

Burns, James M. Roosevelt: the lion and the fox. New York, Harcourt, Brace [1956] 553 p. illus. E807.B835

First inauguration: p. 163-165.
Second inauguration: p. 291-293.
Fourth inauguration: p. 468-469.

1058

Citizens' Joint Committee on National Representation for the District of Columbia. A souvenir of the inauguration of a President of the United States from whose election half-a-million American citizens were barred by constitutional disfranchisement. [Washington, 1933] 16 p. illus. DWP

In F. D. Roosevelt 1933 folder.

1059

Dunn, Charles. Inaugural visitors; cartoons. Democratic bulletin, v. 8, Mar. 1933: 26-27. illus. JK2311.D35, v. 8

1060

Feis, Herbert. 1933: characters in crisis. Boston, Little, Brown [1966] 366 p. E806.F35

First inauguration: p. [95]-97.

1061

Flynn, John T. The Roosevelt myth. Rev. ed. New York, Devin-Adair Co., 1956. 465 p. illus. E807.F59 1956

First inauguration: p. 6-10.
Second inauguration: p. 97.
Third inauguration: p. 233-234.
Fourth inauguration: p. 387.

1062

Front pages from 1314 newspapers entered in the third exhibition of newspaper typography, Ayer Galleries, Philadelphia, 1933. [Philadelphia, 1933] 1 v. (unpaged) PN4867.A1F7 Rare Bk. Coll.

"The newspapers of a Nation, March 4, 1933."

1063

Gillam, William. Some more parades. Mayflower's log, Mar. 1933: 14-15, 35-36, 41-42. illus. F191.W39, 1933

1064

Gilliam, Armistead W. Carrying out the inaugural plans. Sunday star (Washington), Mar. 5, 1933, pt. 7: 8-9, 44. illus. Newsp

1065

High jinks on moving day at the White House. Literary digest, v. 115, Mar. 4, 1933: 34-35. illus. AP2.L58, v. 115

1066

Hurd, Charles. Four fateful inauguration days; the atmosphere of crisis has surrounded Mr. Roosevelt on each historic occasion. New York times magazine, Jan. 14, 1945: 10-11. illus. AP2.N6575, 1945

1067

Inaugural ceremonies to eclipse past celebrations. Mayflower's log, Mar. 1933: 11-12. F191.W39, 1933

1068

The inauguration of the new President of the United States. Illustrated London news, v. 182, Mar. 11, 1933: 327. illus. AP4.I3, v. 182

1069

Inauguration of the President of the United States. Congressional record, 73d Congress, special session of the Senate, v. 77, Mar. 4, 1933: 4-6. J11.R5, v. 77

1070

[Invitation to] the ceremonies attending the inauguration of the President of the United States, March fourth, nineteen hundred thirty-three. [Washington, 1933] folder. DWP

Text on p. [1]. Two portraits laid in.
In F. D. Roosevelt 1933 folder.

1071

Lorant, Stefan. FDR; a pictorial biography. New York, Simon and Schuster, 1950. 159 p. illus., facsims., ports. E807.L78

First inauguration: p. 78-79.
Second inauguration: p. 91.
Third inauguration: p. 111.
Fourth inauguration: p. 135.

1072

Lorentz, Pare, *ed.* The Roosevelt year; a photographic record. New York, Funk & Wagnalls Co., 1934. 197 p. illus., map, ports. (Literary digest books) E806.L65

First inauguration: p. 17-19.

1073

Nesbitt, Victoria H. (Kugler). White House diary, by Henrietta Nesbitt, F. D. R.'s housekeeper. Garden City, N.Y., Doubleday, 1948. 314 p. F204.W5N4

First inauguration: p. 22-23.
Second inauguration: p. 169-174.
Third inauguration: p. 258-259.
Fourth inauguration: p. 303-305.

1074

The new President's call to battle. Literary digest, v. 115, Mar. 11, 1933: 5-7. ports. AP2.L58, v. 115

1075

The 1933 inaugural. Democratic bulletin, v. 8, Feb. 1933: 18-19, 26. port. JK2311.D35, v. 8

1076

Roosevelt, Eleanor (Roosevelt). This I remember. New York, Harper [1949] 387 p. illus., ports. E807.1.R428

First inauguration: p. 77-79.

1077

Roosevelt, Franklin D., *Pres. U.S.* F. D. R.: his personal letters. Foreword by Eleanor Roosevelt; edited by Elliott Roosevelt. New York, Duell, Sloan and Pearce [1947-50] 4 v. illus., facsims., ports. E807.R649

Letters concerning details of first inauguration: v. 3, p. 330-333.

Facsimile of text of his last oath of office, signed by himself and Chief Justice Stone, is given on a plate in v. 4 between p. 1498 and p. 1499.

1078

Roosevelt, James, *and* Sidney Shalett. Affectionately, F. D. R.; a son's story of a lonely man. New York, Harcourt, Brace [1959] 394 p. illus. E807.R657

First inauguration: p. 252-253.
Fourth inauguration: p. 354-356.

1079

Roosevelt takes oath in crisis. News-week, v. 1, Mar. 11, 1933: 8-9. illus. AP2.N6772, v. 1

1080

Rosenman, Samuel I. Working with Roosevelt. New York, Harper [1952] xiv, 560 p. facsims., ports. E807.R73

First inauguration and address: p. 89-91.
Second inauguration and address: p. 142-144.
Third inauguration and address: p. 268-271.
Fourth inauguration and address: p. 516-517.

1081

Schoor, Gene. The picture story of Franklin Delano Roosevelt. New York, Fell, 1950. 94 p. illus., facsims., ports. E807.S3

First inauguration: p. 45-46.
Fourth inauguration: p. 71.

1082

Sherwin, Mark, *and* Charles L. Markmann. Hail to the Chief! *In their* One week in March. New York, Putnam [1961] p. 58-75. illus. D410.5.1933.S5

F. D. Roosevelt's first inauguration.

1083

Sherwood, Robert E. Inaugural parade. Saturday review of literature, v. 9, Mar. 4, 1933: 461-462. Z1219.S25, v. 9

Poem.

1084

Souvenir of Roosevelt & Garner inauguration. [Washington, 1933] [4] p. ports. DWP

In F. D. Roosevelt 1933 folder.

1085

Steinberg, Alfred. Mrs. R, the life of Eleanor Roosevelt. New York, Putnam [1958] 384 p. illus. E807.1.R59

First inauguration: p. 188-189.
Second inauguration: p. 240.
Fourth inauguration: p. 307.

1086

Tully, Grace G. F. D. R., my boss. With a foreword by William O. Douglas. New York, C. Scribner's Sons, 1949. 391 p. E807.T78

Contains scattered references to inaugurations; *see* index.

1087

U.S. *Congress. Joint Committee on Arrangements for the Inauguration, 1933.* Program of the ceremonies attending the inauguration of the President and Vice President of the United States at the National Capitol, March fourth, nineteen thirty-three. Washington, U.S. Govt. Print. Off., 1933. [13] l. DWP

In F. D. Roosevelt 1933 folder.

1088

U.S. *President, 1933-1945 (Franklin D. Roosevelt)* Inaugural address of Franklin D. Roosevelt, President of the United States, delivered at the Capitol, Washington, D. C., March 4, 1933. Washington, U.S. Govt. Print. Off., 1933. 9 p. J82.D61 Mar 4

1089

U.S. *President, 1933-1945 (Franklin D. Roosevelt)* Inaugural address of Franklin D. Roosevelt, President of the United States, delivered at the Capitol, Washington, D.C. March 4, 1933. Washington, U.S. Govt. Print. Off., 1933. 4 p. ([U.S.] 73d Congress, Special session. Senate document 1) J82.D61 Mar. 4a

1090

U.S. *President, 1933-1945 (Franklin D. Roosevelt)* Inaugural addresses of Franklin D. Roosevelt, President of the United States. Washington [U.S. Govt. Print. Off.] 1943. 24 p. E806.U55 1943 Rare Bk. Coll.

1091

U.S. *President, 1933-1945 (Franklin D. Roosevelt)* Inaugural addresses of Franklin D. Roosevelt, President of the United States. The White House, Washington, Christmas 1943. [Washington, U.S. Govt. Print. Off., 1943] 24 p. E806.U55 1943a Rare Bk. Coll.

"One hundred copies ... printed for President Franklin D. Roosevelt."

1092

U.S. *President, 1933-1945 (Franklin D. Roosevelt)* The inaugural addresses of Franklin D. Roosevelt, President of the United States. Worcester, A. J. St. Onge, 1945. 88 p. port. 8 cm. J82.D6 1945a Min. Case

1093

Walker, Turnley. Roosevelt and the Warm Springs story. New York, A. A. Wyn [1953] 311 p. E807.W3

First inauguration: p. 212-214.

1094

Washington, D.C. Inaugural Committee, *1933.* Blue book of the inauguration of Franklin Delano Roosevelt and John Nance Garner as President and Vice President of the United States, March 4, 1933; compiled and edited by the chairman and vice chairman of the Official Program Committee. [Washington] Ransdell [1933?] xvi, 109 p. illus. F199.W31 1933B

1095

Washington, D.C. Inaugural Committee, *1933.* Official program of the inaugural ceremonies inducting into office Franklin D. Roosevelt, President of the United States, John N. Garner, Vice President of the United States, March 4, 1933. [Washington, Ransdell, c1933] 64 p. illus. F199.W31 1933O

Partial contents. The passing of March fourth, by J. Fred Essary (p. 27-30). Inaugural parades of other days, by Ernest G. Walker (p. 35-40). Inaugural balls of the past, by David R. Barbee (p. 55-58).

1096

Washington, D.C. Inaugural Committee, *1933.* Roosevelt-Garner inauguration, March 4, 1933. General Entertainment Committee of the Inaugural Committee. Program of general entertainment. [Washington, 1933?] [4] p. DWP

In F. D. Roosevelt 1933 folder.

1097

"We must act." Time, v. 21, Mar. 13, 1933: 11-12. illus. AP2.T37, v. 29

1098

Wilhelm, G. R. How the telephone helps in inaugurating a President. Transmitter, v. 21, Apr. 1933: 1-6. illus. TK1.T7, v. 21

1099

Wilson, Edmund. Inaugural parade. New republic, v. 74, Mar. 22, 1933: 154-156. AP2.N62, v. 74

Franklin D. Roosevelt Second Inauguration

1100

Bell, William A. Police guard inaugural crowd today. Evening star (Washington), Jan. 20, 1937, inaugural ed.: 23. illus. Newsp

1101

Bolles, Blair. City's hospitality served with skill. Evening star (Washington), Jan. 20, 1937, inaugural ed.: 22. illus. Newsp

About arrangements for receiving and housing inaugural visitors.

1102

CCC marchers, symbol of Roosevelt doctrine, steal the inaugural show. Democratic digest, v. 14, Feb. 1937: 16. JK2311.D35, v. 14

1103

District of Columbia. *Board of Commissioners.* Special regulations, inaugural period, 1937; effective from January 12 to January 28, 1937, both dates inclusive, except as otherwise provided. Washington, U.S. Govt. Print. Off., 1937. 13 p. DWP

In F. D. Roosevelt 1937 folder.

1104

Essary, Helen. Gay luncheon at White House follows rain-drenched inauguration. Democratic digest, v. 14, Feb. 1937: 17.
JK2311.D35, v. 14

1105

44th inauguration of a President; Roosevelt takes office in colorful, simplified ceremony. Literary digest, v. 123, Jan. 23, 1937: 3-4. illus.
AP2.L58, v. 123

1106

Hill, D. William. Behind the scene on inaugural news. Evening star (Washington), Jan. 20, 1937, inaugural ed.: 18. illus. Newsp

1107

If people can take it the President can. Life, v. 2, Feb. 1, 1937: 11-15. illus. AP2.L547, v. 2

1108

Inaugural: soaked dignitaries watch the President 'take it.' News-week, v. 9, Jan. 30, 1937: 11-14. illus. AP2.N6772, v. 9

1109

Inauguration of the President and Vice President of the United States. Congressional record, 75th Congress, 1st session, v. 81, Jan. 21, 1937: 315-318. J11.R5, v. 81

1110

Jacksonian: reinauguration of Roosevelt to stress parallels in two Presidents' careers. Literary digest, v. 122, Dec. 12, 1936: 14-15. illus.
AP2.L58, v. 122

1111

January twentieth at the Capitol of the Nation. Democratic digest, v. 14, Feb. 1937: 10. illus. JK2311.D35, v. 14

Inaugural address reprinted on p. 14-15.

1112

Lloyd, John H. Inaugurating a President. School life, v. 22, Feb. 1937: 163-164. port. L11.S445, v. 22

1113
Martin, Oliver. Inaugurating a President. Transmitter, v. 25, Feb. 1937: 1-6. illus. TK1.T7, v. 25

Installation of telephone and radio broadcasting equipment for the inauguration.

1114
"Mikes" to pick up inauguration. Literary digest, v. 123, Jan. 16, 1937: 30. AP2.L58, v. 123

Preparations for broadcasting the ceremonies.

1115
Mr. Roosevelt's second inauguration. Illustrated London news, v. 190, Feb. 6, 1937: 228. illus. AP4.I3, v. 190

1116
Rishel, Virginia. Happy days are here again, and again ... but Roosevelt's second inaugural will have Jacksonian simplicity. Democratic digest, v. 14, Jan. 1937: 18. JK2311.D35, v. 14

1117
Swearing in the rain. Time, v. 29, Feb. 1, 1937: 9-10. AP2.T37, v. 29

1118
U.S. *President, 1933-1945 (Franklin D. Roosevelt)* Inaugural address of Franklin D. Roosevelt, President of the United States, delivered at the Capitol, Washington, D.C., January 20, 1937. Washington, U.S. Govt. Print. Off., 1937. ix p. J82.D65 Jan. 20

1119
U.S. *President, 1933-1945 (Franklin D. Roosevelt)* Second inaugural address of Franklin D. Roosevelt, President of the United States, delivered at the Capitol, Washington, D.C., January 20, 1937. Washington, U.S. Govt. Print. Off., 1937. 4 p. ([U.S.] 75th Congress, 1st session, Senate document 10) J82.D65 Jan. 20a

1120
Washington, D.C. Inaugural Committee, *1937.* Official program of the inaugural ceremonies inducting into office for a second term Franklin D. Roosevelt, President of the United States, John N. Garner, Vice

President of the United States, January 20, 1937. [Washington, Ransdell, c1937] 56 p. illus. F199.W31 1937O

Partial contents. Why a January 20th inauguration?, by Ruth Finney (p. 29-30). Down the vista of Federal years, by Ernest G. Walker (p. 47-50).

Franklin D. Roosevelt
Third Inauguration

1121

Davies, Joseph E. Plans for the inauguration of the President; radio address. Extension of remarks of Hon. Alben W. Barkley, of Kentucky, in the Senate of the United States, Thursday, December 19 (legislative day of Tuesday, November 19) 1940. Congressional record, 76th Congress, 3d session, v. 86, appendix: 6927-6928. J11.R5, v. 86

1122

Inaugural; pet dog and nervous clerk make history on great day. Life, v. 10, Feb. 3, 1941: 26-30. illus. AP2.L547, v. 10

1123

Inauguration of the President and Vice President of the United States. Congressional record, 77th Congress, 1st session, v. 87, Jan. 20, 1941: 188-190. J11.R5, v. 87

1124

Inauguration of the President and Vice President of the United States of America, Washington, D.C., January 20, 1941. [Ticket to parade stand. Washington, 1941] [2] p. ports. DWP

In F. D. Roosevelt 1941 folder.

1125

Looking at the inauguration from a telephone angle [by] S. T. Transmitter, v. 29, Feb. 1941: 12-13. illus. TK1.T7, v. 29

1126

Major networks arrange record inaugural pickups. Broadcasting, v. 20, Jan. 20, 1941: 16. TK6540.B85, v. 20

1127

Roosevelt calls upon America to defend faith in democracy. Newsweek, v. 17, Jan. 27, 1941: 13-14. illus. AP2.N6772, v. 17

1128

Third term begins. Time, v. 37, Jan. 27, 1941: 11-12. illus.

AP2.T37, v. 37

1129

The third term begins. United States news, v. 10, Jan. 31, 1941: 17. illus.

JK1.U65, v. 10

1130

U.S. *Congress. Joint Committee on Arrangements for the Inauguration, 1941.* Program of the ceremonies attending the inauguration of the President and Vice President of the United States, at the National Capitol, January twentieth, nineteen hundred forty-one. Washington, U.S. Govt. Print. Off., 1941. [8] l. Rare Bk. Coll.

Two portraits laid in.
Broadside portfolio 242, no. 28a.

1131

U.S. *President, 1933-1945 (Franklin D. Roosevelt)* Third inaugural address of Franklin D. Roosevelt, President of the United States, delivered at the Capitol, Washington, D.C., January 20, 1941. Washington, U.S. Govt. Print. Off., 1941. 3 p. ([U.S.] 77th Congress, 1st session. Senate document 6) J82.D69 Jan. 20

1132

Washington, D.C. Inaugural Committee, *1941.* Inaugural gala in honor of the inauguration of President Franklin D. Roosevelt, Vice President Henry A. Wallace ... Sunday, January 19, 1941, Constitution Hall, Washington, D.C. [Washington] H. K. Advertising Press [1941] [14] p. ports. DWP

In F. D. Roosevelt 1941 folder.

1133

Washington, D.C. Inaugural Committee, *1941.* Official program of the ceremonies for the third inauguration of Franklin D. Roosevelt, President of the United States, and the inauguration of Henry A. Wallace, Vice President of the United States, January 20, 1941. [Washington, Ransdell, 1941] 63 p. illus.

E806.W272 Rare Bk. Coll.

Franklin D. Roosevelt
Fourth Inauguration

1134

Albright, Robert C. Backyard inaugural to find oldtimers other side of fence. Washington post, Jan. 14, 1945: B-1. port. Newsp

1135

Carper, Elsie. How FDR out-economized Sen. Byrd. 1945 inaugural: a bargain. Washington post, July 18, 1968: B-1. Newsp

1136

For the fourth time. Time, v. 45, Jan. 29, 1945: 17-19. illus. AP2.T37, v. 45

1137

Four times U.S. President. Illustrated London news, v. 206, Jan. 27, 1945: 102. illus. AP4.I3, v. 206

1138

Hail to the Chief. Newsweek, v. 25, Jan. 29, 1945: 40-41. illus. AP2.N6772, v. 25

1139

Hail to the Chief–the fourth term begins. Democratic digest, v. 22, Feb. 1945: 7-10. illus. JK2311.D35, v. 22

Another illustration on cover.

1140

Inaugural airing held down by nets. Broadcasting, v. 28, Jan. 22, 1945: 62. TK6540.B85, v. 28

1141

Inauguration ceremonies. Congressional record, 79th Congress, 1st session, v. 91, Jan. 22, 1945: 364-365. J11.R5, v. 91

1142

Life goes to inauguration; ceremony is simple but high jinks around it are gay and expensive. Life, v. 18, Feb. 5, 1945: 108-110, 113. illus. AP2.L547, v. 18

1143

U.S. *President, 1933-1945 (Franklin D. Roosevelt)* Fourth inaugural address of Franklin D. Roosevelt, President of the United States, delivered on the portico of the White House, Washington, D.C., together with the invocation and benediction, January 20, 1945. Washington, U.S. Govt. Print. Off., 1945. 5 p. ([U.S.] 79th Congress, 1st session. Senate document 40) J82.D695 Jan. 20b

Harry S. Truman

1144

Asbell, Bernard. When F. D. R. died. New York, Holt, Rinehart and Winston [1961] 211 p. illus. E807.A85

Truman's inauguration: p. 106-109.

1145

Clemens, Cyril. The man from Missouri, a biography of Harry S. Truman. Webster Groves, Mo., International Mark Twain Society; J. P. Didier, Distributors, New York, 1945. 184 p. facsims., ports. E814.C55

Inauguration: p. 128-133.

1146

McNaughton, Frank, *and* Walter Hehmeyer. This man Truman. New York, Whittlesey House, McGraw-Hill Book Co. [1945] 219 p. plates (part col.), ports. E814.M3

Inauguration: p. 207-211.

1147

The new President, Mr. Harry S. Truman, being sworn in by Chief Justice Harlan Fiske Stone. Illustrated London news, v. 206, Apr. 21, 1945: 423. illus. AP4.I3, v. 206

1148

Phillips, Cabell B. H. The Truman Presidency; the history of a triumphant succession. New York, Macmillan [1966] 463 p. illus., ports. E813.P5 1966

First inauguration: p. 6-7.
Second inaugural address: p. 266-267, 272-273.
Eisenhower's first inauguration: p. 429-431.

1149

Steinberg, Alfred. The man from Missouri: the life and times of Harry S. Truman. New York, G. P. Putnam's Sons [1962] 447 p. E814.S74

First inauguration: p. 234-235.
Second inauguration: p. 334-335.

1150
The thirty-second. Time, v. 45, Apr. 23, 1945: 21. illus. AP2.T37, v. 45

1151
Truman, Harry S., *Pres. U.S.* Memoirs. Garden City, N.Y., Doubleday, 1955-56. 2 v. E814.T75

Contents. v. 1. Year of decisions. v. 2. Years of trial and hope.
First inauguration: v. 1, p. 6-8.
Second inauguration and excerpts from address: v. 2, p. 225-229.

1152
Truman, Margaret. Souvenir, Margaret Truman's own story; by Margaret Truman, with Margaret Cousins. New York, McGraw-Hill [1956] 365 p. illus. E814.1.T7

First inauguration: p. 86.
Second inauguration: p. 252-254.

1153
Truman sworn in in the White House; he becomes 33rd President. Life, v. 18, Apr. 23, 1945: 28-29. illus. AP2.L547, v. 18

1154
U.S. closes ranks under Truman after shock of Roosevelt's death. Newsweek, v. 25, Apr. 23, 1945: 26-27. illus. AP2.N6772, v. 25

Harry S. Truman
Second Inauguration

1155
The announcement of United States world policy; and the Washington ceremonies attending the inauguration of President Truman's first elected term of office. Illustrated London news, v. 214, Jan. 29, 1949: 135. illus. AP4.I3, v. 214

1156
Association of American Railroads. Inaugural train information for the press and radio. Washington [1949?] 7 l. DWP

In Truman inauguration scrapbook.

325-882 O-69—12

1157

Daly, John J. Television and the inauguration. National republic, v. 36, Jan. 1949: 3-4. ports. E171.N32, v. 36

1158

District of Columbia. *Board of Commissioners.* [Special regulations for the preservation of public order and the protection of life and property in connection with the Presidential inaugural ceremonies in 1949] Washington, 1948. 8 l. DWP

In Truman inauguration scrapbook.

1159

Fashion: for the ladies. Newsweek, v. 33, Jan. 24, 1949: 17. illus. AP2.N6772, v. 33

Describes gowns to be worn by Mrs. Truman and Margaret Truman at inaugural functions.

1160

Hail to the Chief. Democratic digest, v. 26, Feb./Mar. 1949: 3-4. JK2311.D35, v. 26

Illustrations on p. 12-13.

1161

Happy days are here again! Commonweal, v. 49, Dec. 24, 1948: 268. AP2.C6897, v. 49

Plans for celebrating President Truman's inaugural.

1162

I have the job. Time, v. 53, Jan. 31, 1949: 16-17. illus. AP2.T37, v. 53

1163

Inaugural ink. Newsweek, v. 33, Jan. 31, 1949: 51-52. illus. AP2.N6772, v. 33

Reporting the inauguration.

1164

Inaugural tests TV; coverage success despite technical problems. Broadcasting, telecasting, v. 36, Jan. 24, 1949: 63. TK6540.B85, v. 36

1165
The inauguration. American federationist, v. 56, Feb. 1949: 16-17. illus.
HD8055.A5A2, v. 56

1166
Inauguration by video. Newsweek, v. 33, Jan. 31, 1949: 49.
AP2.N6772, v. 33

1167
Inauguration: coverage plans final; music cleared. Broadcasting, telecasting, v. 36, Jan. 17, 1949: 24. plan. TK6540.B85, v. 36

1168
Inauguration newsreel; history through photographs. U.S. news & world report, v. 26, Jan. 28, 1949: 16-17. illus. JK1.U65, v. 26

1169
Inauguration of the President and Vice President of the United States. Congressional record, 81st Congress, 1st session, v. 95, Jan. 20, 1949: 476-479. J11.R5, v. 95

1170
[Invitation to] the inauguration of the President of the United States, January twentieth, nineteen hundred forty-nine. [Washington, 1949] 1 p. DWP

In Truman inauguration scrapbook.

1171
Kennedy, George. Battery D here for inaugural of its World War I commander. Evening star (Washington), Jan. 19, 1949: A-1.
Newsp

1172
Kennedy, George. Five sets of television cameras to send out inaugural scenes. Evening star (Washington), Jan. 18, 1949: A-4. illus.
Newsp

1173
The march of the little fellows. Newsweek, v. 33, Jan. 31, 1949: 15-18. illus. AP2.N6772, v. 33

1174

Museums and the Truman inauguration. Museum news (Washington, D.C.), v. 26, Feb. 15, 1949: 1. AM1.A55, v. 26

1175

O'Donnell, James F. "I, Harry S. Truman, do solemnly swear ..." How millions heard and saw the inauguration through the magic of radio and television, aided by telephone equipment and know-how. Transmitter, v. 37, Mar./Apr. 1949: 4-10. illus. TK1.T7, v. 37

1176

Osbon, John. Capital ceremonies: radio, video coverage unprecedented. Broadcasting, telecasting, v. 36, Jan. 24, 1949: 24-25, 63-64. illus. TK6540.B85, v. 36

1177

The President hopes to be present. New York times, Jan. 15, 1949: 2. illus. Newsp

Reproduces official invitation to President and Mrs. Truman with his reply written on it.

1178

Sancton, Thomas. Truman's big parade. Nation v. 168, Jan. 29, 1949: 120-121. AP2.N2, v. 168

1179

Television covers its first inaugural. Washington post, Jan. 20, 1949: 3. Newsp

1180

32d President of the U.S. takes over biggest peacetime government. U.S. news & world report, v. 26, Jan. 21, 1949: 11-13. illus. JK1.U65, v. 26

1181

Truman is inaugurated. Life, v. 26, Jan. 31, 1949: 15-25. illus. AP2.L547, v. 26

1182

U.S. *Congress. Joint Committee on Arrangements for the Inauguration, 1949.* Program of the ceremonies attending the inauguration of the

President and Vice President of the United States at the National Capitol, January twentieth, nineteen hundred forty-nine. Washington, U.S. Govt. Print. Off., 1949. [8] l. DWP

In Truman folder.

1183

U.S. *President, 1945-1953 (Truman)* Inaugural address delivered at the Capitol, Washington, D.C., January 20, 1949. Washington, U.S. Govt. Print. Off., 1949. 5 p. ([U.S.] 81st Congress, 1st session, 1949. Senate document no. 5) J82.D75 Jan. 20

1184

Units in the inaugural parade. Army, Navy and Air Force register, v. 70, Jan. 22, 1949: 15. U1.A8, v. 70

1185

Washington, D.C. Inaugural Committee, *1949.* Appointing archivist to Inaugural Committee and prescribing his duties. [Washington] 1948. 1 l. (*Its* Mimeo, no. 17) DWP

In Truman inauguration scrapbook.

1186

Washington, D.C. Inaugural Committee, *1949.* Inaugural events. Rev. Jan. 15, 1949. [Washington] 1949. 5 l. (*Its* Mimeo, no. 142) DWP

In Truman inauguration scrapbook.

1187

Washington, D.C. Inaugural Committee, *1949.* Official program commemorating the inauguration of Harry S. Truman, President of the United States of America, and Alben W. Barkley, Vice President of the United States of America. [Limited de luxe ed. Washington] 1949. 72 p. illus. F199.W31 1949O Rare Bk. Coll.

1188

Washington, D.C. Inaugural Committee, *1949.* Preservation of records of the committee. [Washington] 1948. 2 l. (*Its* Mimeo, no. 18) DWP

In Truman inauguration scrapbook.

1189

Washington, D.C. Inaugural Committee, *1949.* Program. State groups activities during inauguration period. [Washington, 1949] 7 l. (*Its* Mimeo, no. 127) DWP

In Truman folder.

1190

Washington, D.C. Office of the Grand Marshal, *1949.* Inaugural parade, 20 January 1949. [Washington, 1949] 39 l. maps. (General orders, no. 1) F199.W31 1949g

1191

Washington sets stage for inaugural. Democratic digest, v. 25, Dec. 1948/Jan. 1949: 15. illus. JK2311.D35, v. 25

Dwight D. Eisenhower

1192

Adams, Sherman. Firsthand report; the story of the Eisenhower administration. New York, Harper [1961] 481 p. illus. E835.A3

First inauguration: p. 66-70.

1193

Air safety group protests plan to fly 460 planes at inaugural. New York herald-tribune, Jan. 10, 1953: 1, 18. Newsp

1194

Big fly-by; military air show is set for inaugural parade. Aviation week, v. 58, Jan. 19, 1953: 16-17. TL501.A8, v. 58

1195

Brandon, Dorothy (Barrett). Mamie Doud Eisenhower; a portrait of a First Lady. New York, Scribner, 1954. 307 p. illus. E837.E4B7

First inauguration: p. 306-307.

1196

Brown, John Mason. Through these men; some aspects of our passing history. New York, Harper [1956] 302 p. E835.B7

Eisenhower's first inauguration: p. 51-56.

1197

Brown, John Mason. The Trumans leave the White House. Saturday review, v. 36, Feb. 7, 1953: 9-11, 47-49. illus. Z1219.S25, v. 36

1198

Davidson, Robert H. While millions watched and listened, a President took office. Transmitter, v. 41, Mar./Apr. 1953: 2-4, 65-66. illus. TK1.T7, v. 41

1199

Donovan, Robert J. From the Commodore to the White House. *In his* Eisenhower: the inside story. New York, Harper [1956] p. 1-23. ports. E835.D6

Tells about the drafting of Eisenhower's inaugural address, preparations for the inauguration, and the events of inauguration day.

1200

Eisenhower, Dwight D., *Pres. U.S.* Mandate for change, 1953-1956; the White House years. Garden City, N.Y., Doubleday, 1963. xviii, 650 p. illus., maps (part col.), ports. E835.E33

First inauguration: p. 100-103.

1201

Eisenhower, Dwight D., *Pres. U.S.* The prayer of Dwight D. Eisenhower, preceding his inaugural address as 34th President of the United States of America, January 20, 1953. [New York, Printed at the Hammer Creek Press, 1953] [4] p. E836.A56 Rare Bk. Coll.

1202

Faith & freedom. Prayer & preparation. Time, v. 61, Jan. 26, 1953: 17-18. illus. AP2.T37, v. 61

First article quotes passages from Eisenhower's prayer and inaugural address; second includes information about Bibles used and passages on which President intended to place his hand when taking the oath.

1203

Great day. Time, v. 61, Feb. 2, 1953: 12-13. illus. AP2.T37, v. 61

1204

Hughes, Emmet J. The ordeal of power; a political memoir of the Eisenhower years. New York, Atheneum, 1963. 372 p.
E835.H8 1963

First inauguration: p. 55-56.
Second inauguration: p. 230-234.

1205

Inaugural bid at last loses sorrow sign. Washington post, Jan. 18, 1953: 15M. illus. Newsp

Official invitation is redesigned.

1206

The inaugural: biggest and best. Newsweek, v. 41, Jan. 12, 1953: 18. illus.
AP2.N6772, v. 41

1207

Inaugural Committee to provide advice for its successors. Sunday star (Washington), Feb. 1, 1953: A-12. Newsp

1208

Inaugural in a goldfish bowl: radio-TV blanket ceremonies. Broadcasting, telecasting, v. 44, Jan. 26, 1953: 39. illus. TK6540.B85, v. 44

1209

Inaugural lumber for souvenirs. Evening star (Washington), Feb. 4, 1953: A-15. illus. Newsp

1210

The inaugural reviewing stand. *In* American Institute of Architects. Journal, v. 19, Mar. 1953: 117-118. NA1.A326, v. 19

Illustration on p. 116.

1211

Inaugural vs. coronation: democracy is cheaper. New York times, Oct. 16, 1952: 22. Newsp

A comparison of the prices for seats to view the processions.

1212

Inauguration. Time, v. 61, Jan. 12, 1953: 17-18. illus. AP2.T37, v. 61

Report on preparations for Eisenhower's inauguration includes brief review of some notable past inaugurations.

1213

Inauguration eye-view. Vogue, v. 121, Feb. 15, 1953: 88. TT500.V7, v. 121

1214

1214

The inauguration of President Eisenhower. Illustrated London news, v. 222, Jan. 31, 1953: 154-155. illus. AP4.I3, v. 222

1215

Inauguration of President of the United States and Vice President. Congressional record, 83d Congress, 1st session, v. 99, Jan. 20, 1953: 450-452. J11.R5, v.99

1216

Inauguration of the President and Vice President of the United States of America, Washington, D.C., January 20, 1953. [Ticket to parade stand. Washington, 1953] 1 p. DWP

In Eisenhower 1953 folder.

1217

It couldn't have happened anyplace else in the world. Life, v. 34, Feb. 2, 1953: 14-22. illus. AP2.L547, v. 34

Color photograph of inauguration scene appears on cover of this issue.

1218

MacArthur, Harry. Inauguration believed viewed by 70 million on TV screens. Evening star (Washington), Jan. 21, 1953: A-12. Newsp

1219

Mr. Six sees an inauguration. Business week, Jan. 31, 1953: 30-32. illus. HF5001.B89, 1953

1220

Nation off to a fresh start as Eisenhower takes the helm. Newsweek, v. 41, Jan. 26, 1953: 25-27. illus. AP2.N6772, v. 41

1221

Pattee, Dorothea. Inaugural simple or gala? The decision is up to Ike. Washington post, Nov. 9, 1952: 1S. illus. Newsp

1222

Photo report: inauguration, U.S. style. U.S. news & world report, v. 34, Jan. 30, 1953: 29-32. illus. JK1.U65, v. 34

Text of inaugural address appears on p. 98-99.

1223

Pusey, Merlo J. Eisenhower, the President. New York, Macmillan, 1956. 300 p. E835.P8

Eisenhower's inaugural prayer: p. 105-107.

1224

Radio, TV to shoot the works in covering inauguration. Broadcasting, telecasting, v. 44, Jan. 19, 1953: 37, 40. illus. TK6540.B85, v. 44

1225

Reston, James. Eisenhower lowers boom on top hat, elects a homburg. New York times, Jan. 15, 1953: 20. illus. Newsp

1226

Rovere, Richard H. Letter from Washington. New Yorker, v. 28, Jan. 31, 1953: 55-60. AP2.N6763, v. 28

Reprinted as chapter 9, "Inauguration," in his *The Eisenhower Years; Affairs of State* (New York, Farrar, Straus and Cudahy [1956] E835.R6), p. 74-80.

1227

Seldes, Gilbert. Notes on an event. Saturday review, v. 36, Feb. 7, 1953: 28. Z1219.S25, v. 36

About television coverage.

1228

Snyder, Marty. My friend Ike, by Marty Snyder, with Glenn D. Kittler. New York, F. Fell, 1956. 237 p. illus. E836.S58

First inauguration: p. 195-197.

1229

Stein, Sonia. 75 million TV viewers may see inaugural. Washington post, Jan. 18, 1953: 1L. Newsp

1230

Truman, Harry S., *Pres. U.S.* The day Ike snubbed me. Look, v. 24, May 24, 1960: 25-33. illus. AP2.L79, v. 24

Published in somewhat different form in his *Mr. Citizen* ([New York] Geis Associates, distributed by Random House [1960] E814.A33), p. 15-23.

1231

U.S. *President, 1953-1961 (Eisenhower)* Inaugural address delivered at the Capitol, Washington, D.C., January 20, 1953. Washington, U.S. Govt. Print. Off., 1953. 5 p. ([U.S.] 83d Congress, 1st session. Senate document no. 9) J82.D81 Jan. 20

1232

Unna, Warren. Elephants, musicians, medals and Bible ride inaugural merry-go-round. Washington post, Dec. 19, 1952: 29. ports. Newsp

1233

Unna, Warren. A 'simple' inaugural–no firecrackers. Washington post, Jan. 20, 1953, special inaugural section: 15. Newsp

1234

Waiting for inauguration day. Business week, Jan. 17, 1953: 28-29. illus. HF5001.B89, 1953

1235

Washington, D.C. Inaugural Committee, *1953.* Complimentary guide book. [Washington, 1953?] 64 p. illus., maps, ports. DWP

In Eisenhower 1953 folder.

1236

Washington, D.C. Inaugural Committee, *1953.* Official program of the inaugural ceremonies inducting into office Dwight D. Eisenhower, President of the United States [and] Richard M. Nixon, Vice President of the United States, January 20, 1953. [Washington, 1953] 48 p. illus. F199.W31 1953

Copy also in DWP, in Eisenhower 1953 folder.

1237

Washington, D.C. Office of the Grand Marshals, *1953*. Inaugural parade, 20 January 1953. [Washington, U.S. Govt. Print. Off., 1953] 60 p. plans. (General orders, no. 1) DWP

Change 1, General Order No. 1 ([4] p.) laid in.
In Eisenhower 1953 folder.

1238

Wilson, Jack. When you are President you stand up and smile. Look, v. 17, Jan. 13, 1953: 76. AP2.L79, v. 17

1239

Wilson, Jack. You have to love horses to run an inauguration.. Look, v. 17, Jan. 27, 1953: 96. AP2.L79, v. 17

1240

Wood, Robert H. Sage decision for safety. Aviation week, v. 58, Feb. 2, 1953: 102. TL501.A8, v. 58

Comments on the cancellation of the inauguration fly-by over the District of Columbia.

Dwight D. Eisenhower
Second Inauguration

1241

Capital starts cleanup after inaugural hoopla. Washington post, Jan. 23, 1957: B-1. Newsp

1242

Capitol carillons to announce the moment of inauguration. New York times, Jan. 13, 1957: 50. Newsp

1243

Casey, Phil. Amendment ends old inauguration gap. Washington post, Dec. 16, 1956: A-2. port. Newsp

Refers to the 20th amendment to the Constitution.

1244

Dean, Ruth. For inaugural, invitations pose knotty problems. Evening star (Washington), Jan. 21, 1957: B-4, B-7. illus. Newsp

1245
Delaware in lead again; to head shortened inaugural parade as 'her right.' New York times, Dec. 9, 1956: 74. Newsp

1246
Eisenhower, Dwight D., *Pres. U.S.* Waging peace, 1956-1961; the White House years. Garden City, N.Y., Doubleday, 1965. xxiii, 741 p. illus., ports. E835.E47

Second inauguration: p. 103.
Excerpt from address: p. 101.

1247
Flashback. Washington post, Jan. 25, 1957: A-3. illus. Newsp

Shows private oath-taking ceremony held on Jan. 20, 1957.

1248
Fleeson, Doris. The President's swearing-in: dim view taken of plan to keep Sunday oath-taking private. Evening star (Washington), Jan. 17, 1957: A-9. Newsp

1249
Folliard, Edward T. Ike, Nixon take oath in private. Washington post, Jan. 21, 1957: A-1, A-3. Newsp

Account of the private oath-taking ceremony held on Sunday, Jan. 20, from which the press was excluded.

1250
Fourth faith. Newsweek, v. 49, Feb. 4, 1957: 86. AP2.N6772, v. 49

For the first time, a representative of the Greek Orthodox Church participates in the inauguration ceremonies.

1251
Harrison, Bernie. Another inaugural on TV. Sunday star (Washington), Televue, Jan. 20, 1957: 1-2. illus. Newsp

1252
Homburg is 'king' for the inaugural. Sunday star (Washington), Jan. 20, 1957: C-2. illus. Newsp

1253
Inauguration. New Yorker, v. 32, Feb. 2, 1957: 26-27. AP2.N6763, v. 32

1254

Inauguration medals ready. Washington post, Dec. 26, 1956: A-8. illus.
Newsp

1255

Inauguration of the President and Vice President of the United States. Congressional record, 85th Congress, 1st session, v. 103, Jan. 21, 1957: 804-806. J11.R5, v. 103

1256

Inauguration photo report: as Ike starts second term. U.S. news & world report, v. 42, Feb. 1, 1957: 52-55. illus. JK1.U65, v. 42

1257

Inauguration takes over Capital. Business week, Jan. 12, 1957: 109-110. illus. HF5001.B89, 1957

1258

Kerr protests putting Indians at parade's end. Washington post, Jan. 27, 1957: B-4. Newsp

1259

Langbein, F. W. Teamwork played its part in good communications for the inauguration of a President. Transmitter, v. 45, Mar./Apr. 1957: 2-5. illus. TK1.T7, v. 45

1260

Lawrence, David. Inauguration a symbol of equality; bi-racial and multi-religious roles in services seen as signal to world. Evening star (Washington), Jan. 23, 1957: A-21. Newsp

1261

Let joy be unconfined. Reporter, v. 16, Jan. 24, 1957: 2, 4.
D839.R385, v. 16

Preparing for the inauguration.

1262

Lewine, Frances. Inauguration costs $1 million; a mere 35 words makes it legal. Washington post, Jan. 21, 1957: C-15. Newsp

1263
McLendon, Winzola. Service splendor for the 'big parade.' Diplomat, v. 8, Jan. 1957: 39, 65. ports. AP2.D575, v. 8

1264
Networks firm details of inaugural coverage. Broadcasting, telecasting, v. 52, Jan. 21, 1957: 88. TK6540.B85, v. 52

1265
President Eisenhower's second term: inauguration ceremonies. Illustrated London news, v. 230, Feb. 2, 1957: 187. illus. AP4.I3, v. 230

1266
Presidential oath videotaped. Broadcasting, telecasting, v. 52, Jan. 28, 1957: 68. illus. TK6540.B85, v. 52

1267
Resume of the inaugural round. Diplomat, v. 8, Jan. 1957: 36-37. AP2.D575, v. 8

1268
Second inaugural. "Beyond our own frontiers." Time, v. 69, Jan. 28, 1957: 17-18. illus. AP2.T37, v. 69

Includes excerpts from the inaugural address.

1269
A solemn inaugural and a gay celebration. Life, v. 42, Feb. 4, 1957: 24-33. illus. AP2.L547, v. 42

1270
The sun comes out. New republic, v. 136, Feb. 4, 1957: 2. AP2.N624, v. 136

1271
U.S. *President, 1953-1961 (Eisenhower)* Inaugural address delivered at the Capitol, Washington, D.C., January 21, 1957. Washington, U.S. Govt. Print. Off., 1957. 4 p. ([U.S.] 85th Congress, 1st session. Senate document no. 15) J82.D85 Jan. 21

1272
U.S. *President, 1953-1961 (Eisenhower)* The price of peace; second

inaugural address delivered at the Capitol, January 21, 1957. [Washington, U.S. Govt. Print. Off., 1957] 9 p. (U.S. Dept. of State. Publication 6415. General foreign policy series, 114) E835.U565

1273

Washington, D.C. Inaugural Committee, *1957.* Inauguration 1957 guide book. [Washington, 1957?] 29 p. illus., maps, ports. DWP

Two copies in Eisenhower 1957 folder.

1274

Washington, D.C. Inaugural Committee, *1957.* Official program, 43rd inauguration, 1957; inducting into office, Dwight D. Eisenhower, President of the United States [and] Richard M. Nixon, Vice President of the United States. [Washington, 1957] 48 p. illus. F199.W31 1957

Two copies also in DWP, in Eisenhower 1957 folder.

John F. Kennedy

1275

Beerless inauguration. America, v. 104, Jan. 28, 1961: 554. BX801.A5, v. 104

Refers to sponsorship of television broadcasts.

1276

Byron, George H. Telephone men and women again meet inaugural communications challenge. Transmitter, v. 49, Jan./Feb. 1961: 2-4. illus. TK1.T7, v. 49

1277

Childs, Marquis W. Unique aspects of the inaugural. Washington post, Jan. 20, 1961: A-20. Newsp

1278

The 44th inaugural. The 'second family.' Newsweek, v. 57, Jan. 30, 1961: 18-19. illus. AP2.N6772, v. 57

1279

Frost, Robert. Dedication [and] The gift outright [by Robert Frost] The inaugural address [of John Fitzgerald Kennedy] Washington, D.C.,

January the twentieth, 1961. [New York, Printed for friends of the Spiral Press, 1961] [19] l. illus. PS3511.R94D4 Rare Bk. Coll.

"Edition ... of five hundred copies ... This copy is number 291."

The poems were "presented as part of the inaugural ceremonies, January the twentieth, 1961."

1280

Inaugural: a big job in a short time. Democratic digest, v. 8, Jan./Feb. 1961: 48-49. port. JK2311.D34, v. 8

1281

The inauguration: 1961. Commonweal, v. 73, Feb. 3, 1961: 471-472. AP2.C6897, v. 73

1282

Inauguration of the President of the United States and Vice President. Congressional record, 87th Congress, 1st session, v. 107, Jan. 20, 1961: 1010-1013. J11.R5, v. 107

1283

[Invitation] to attend and participate in the inauguration of John Fitzgerald Kennedy. [Washington, 1961] 1 p. DWP

In Kennedy inauguration scrapbook.

1284

Johnson, Haynes. Here's how Kennedy wrote own speech. Evening star (Washington), Jan. 22, 1961: A-1, A-6. Newsp

1285

Kennedy crew to ride PT boat at inaugural. Washington post, Dec. 11, 1960: B-1. Newsp

1286

Lasky, Victor. J. F. K.: the man and the myth. New York, Macmillan [1963] 653 p. E842.L3

Inauguration: p. 19-23.

1287

Lewis, Anthony. Presidential diary: Kennedy's day is long, exhilerating and occasionally tedious. New York times, Jan. 21, 1961: 11. illus. Newsp

325-882 O-69—13

1288

Life *(Chicago)* Inaugural spectacle, by the editors of Life. Souvenir ed. [New York? c1961] [67] p. illus. F200.L5

1289

Lincoln, Evelyn. My twelve years with John F. Kennedy. New York, D. McKay Co. [1965] 371 p. E842.L54

Inauguration: p. 223-227.

1290

Lowe, Jacques. The inauguration, 1961. *In his* Portrait: the emergence of John F. Kennedy. New York, McGraw-Hill [1961] p. 196-223. illus., ports. E842.L65

1291

McGrory, Mary. Flying start and notable agility. America, v. 104, Feb. 4, 1961: 585. BX801.A5, v. 104

1292

Markmann, Charles L., *and* Mark Sherwin. The inauguration. *In their* John F. Kennedy: a sense of purpose. New York, St. Martin's Press [1961] p. 82-89. E841.M3

1293

Meyers, Joan S., *ed.* John Fitzgerald Kennedy; as we remember him. Edited and produced under the direction of Goddard Lieberson. Editor, Joan Meyers; art director, Ira Teichberg. New York, Atheneum, 1965. illus., facsims., group ports. (A Columbia records legacy collection book) E842.M46

Inauguration: p. 107-[113].

1294

New era–photo report. John F. Kennedy, President of the United States. U.S. news & world report, v. 50, Jan. 30, 1961: 32-36. illus. JK1.U65, v. 50

1295

A new hand, a new voice, a new verve. Life, v. 50, Jan. 27, 1961: 16-30. illus. AP2.L547, v. 50

Color photograph of President's drive to White House after inauguration appears on cover of this issue.

1296

New York times. The Kennedy years. Text prepared under the direction of Harold Faber with contributions by John Corry [and others] Introduction by Tom Wicker. Photographs by Jacques Lowe and others. Contributing photographer: George Tames. New York, Viking Press [1964] 327 p. illus. (part col.), ports. (part col.) E842.N45

Inauguration: p. 149-[172].

1297

Robert Frost adds poet's touch. New York times, Jan. 21, 1961: 9. illus. Newsp

Gives text of "Preface" and "The Gift Outright."

1298

Schlesinger, Arthur M., *Jr.* A thousand days; John F. Kennedy in the White House. Boston, Houghton Mifflin Co., 1965. xiv, 1087 p. E841.S3

Inauguration: p. [1]-5, 164-165, 731-732.

1299

Sidey, Hugh. John F. Kennedy, President. New York, Atheneum, 1963. 400 p. E842.S5

Inauguration: p. 37-42.

1300

Sorensen, Theodore C. Kennedy. New York, Harper & Row [1965] 783 p. port. E841.S6

Inauguration and address: p. 240-248.

1301

Special report on inauguration; historic installation of John Kennedy saw more Negro participation than any other in history. Ebony, v. 16, Mar. 1961: 33-38, 40-41, 88-90. illus. (part col.) AP2.E165, v. 16

1302

Text of 4 prayers at Capitol ceremony. New York times, Jan. 21, 1961: 12. Newsp

1303

U.S. *President, 1961-1963 (Kennedy)* The first book edition of John F. Kennedy's inaugural address. Proclamation by Lyndon B. Johnson. Illustrated by Leonard Everett Fisher. New York, F. Watts [1964] 39 p. illus. J82.D91 Jan 20c

1304

U.S. *President, 1961-1963 (Kennedy)* The inaugural address, by John F. Kennedy, January 20, 1961. Washington, Colortone Press [1965?] 1 v. (unpaged) illus. J82.D91 Jan. 20d 1965

1305

U.S. *President, 1961-1963 (Kennedy)* Inaugural address delivered at the Capitol, Washington, D.C., January 20, 1961. Washington, U.S. Govt. Print. Off., 1961. 3 p. ([U.S.] 87th Congress, 1st session. Senate document no. 9) J82.D91 Jan. 20

1306

U.S. *President, 1961-1963 (Kennedy)* The inaugural address, delivered at the Capitol, Washington, January 20, 1961. Worcester, A. J. St. Onge [1961] 30 p. port. 68 mm. J82.D91 Jan. 20a Min. Case

1307

U.S. *President, 1961-1963 (Kennedy)* Inaugural address of John Fitzgerald Kennedy, 35th President of the United States, delivered at the Capitol, Washington, January 20, 1961. [Los Angeles, 1965] 47 p. port. 43 mm. J82.D91 Jan. 20b Min. Case

"Handset, printed and bound by Bela Blau, Los Angeles, California, January 20, 1965."

1308

U.S. *President, 1961-1963 (Kennedy)* Inaugural address of John Fitzgerald Kennedy, Thirty-fifth President of the United States of America, Washington, D.C., Inauguration Day: 20 January 1961. [Los Angeles? 1961?] 13 p. J82.D91 Jan. 20b Rare Bk. Coll.

"Printed by students of 'The Art of the Book' at the Press of the Department of Fine Arts, University of Southern California."

1309

Washington, D.C. Inaugural Committee, *1961.* The inauguration of John Fitzgerald Kennedy and Lyndon Baines Johnson, January 20,

1961. Edward H. Foley, chairman. Samuel C. Brightman, director of publicity. [John P. Anderson, editor. Washington, 1962?] 1 v. (unpaged) illus. F200.W28 Rare Bk. Coll.

Reproductions of articles, illustrations, etc., chiefly from American and foreign newspapers.

1310

Washington, D.C. Inaugural Committee, *1961.* Official program, inaugural ceremonies of John F. Kennedy, thirty-fifth President of the United States, and Lyndon B. Johnson, thirty-seventh Vice President of the United States. Washington, D.C., January 20, 1961. [Washington] c1961. 63 p. illus. F200.W3

Partial contents. Colorful inaugurals of the past, by Frederick B. Sweet (p. 40-42). The inaugural ball, past and present (p. [50]).

1311

Washington, D.C. Inaugural Committee, *1961.* Official program: inaugural ceremonies of John F. Kennedy, thirty-fifth President of the United States, and Lyndon B. Johnson, thirty-seventh Vice President of the United States. Washington, D.C., January 20, 1961. [Washington, 1961] 63, 31 p. illus. F200.W314 Rare Bk. Coll.

"A Pictorial Review: 1961 Inauguration, Including the Complete Text of the Presidential Inaugural Address" (31 p. at end) has special title page.

"Copy no. 120 of the limited deluxe edition."

1312

"We shall pay any price." The 35th. Time, v. 77, Jan. 27, 1961: 7-12. illus. AP2.T37, v. 77

Box on p. 8 contains excerpts from the inaugural address.

1313

West, Dick. Frost wrote inauguration poetry fast. Washington post, Jan. 27, 1961: A-6. Newsp

1314

Wolfarth, Donald L. John F. Kennedy in the tradition of inaugural speeches. Quarterly journal of speech, v. 47, Apr. 1961: 124-132. tables. PN4071.Q3, v. 47

First table, on p. 125, shows number of words and sentences in inaugural addresses.

Lyndon B. Johnson

1315

Amrine, Michael. This awesome challenge, the hundred days of Lyndon Johnson. New York, Putnam [1964] 283 p. E846.A6

Inauguration: p. 23-25.

1316

Blumenthal, Fred. This week's inauguration recalls 30 seconds of history. Parade, Jan. 17, 1965: 10. illus. AP2.P263, 1965

About the swearing in of President Johnson on Nov. 22, 1963.

1317

The day Kennedy died. Newsweek, v. 62, Dec. 2, 1963: 20-26. illus. AP2.N6772, v. 62

Includes an account of the swearing in (p. 24-25) and a photograph of the ceremony (p. 22).

1318

The full record. Time, v. 89, Feb. 24, 1967: 19-21. illus. AP2.T37, v. 89

A series of photographs taken when President Johnson was sworn in on Nov. 22, 1963.

1319

"I ask your help—and God's." Life, v. 55, Nov. 29, 1963: 30-31. illus. AP2.L547, v. 55

President Johnson is sworn in.

1320

Knebel, Fletcher. After the shots: the ordeal of Lyndon Johnson. Look, v. 28, Mar. 10, 1964: 26-28, 30, 33. port. AP2.L79, v. 28

Includes description of the swearing-in ceremony.

1321

Manchester, William R. The death of a President, November 20—November 25, 1963. New York, Harper & Row [1967] xvi, 710 p. E842.9.M28 1967

Swearing in of President Johnson: p. 324-326.

1322

Mr. Johnson is sworn in as the 36th President. Illustrated London news, v. 243, Nov. 30, 1963: 890. illus. AP4.I3, v. 243

1323

A new President is sworn in at a time of stress and tragedy, by a woman, Judge Sarah Hughes. Congressional record, 88th Congress, 1st session, v. 109, Dec. 4, 1963: 23212-23213. J11.R5, v. 109

Reprints article by Judge Hughes which originally appeared in the *Texas Observer* of Nov. 29, 1963.

1324

New York times. The road to the White House; the story of the 1964 election, by the staff of the New York times. Edited by Harold Faber. New York, McGraw-Hill [1965] xvi, 305 p. illus., ports. E850.N42

Johnson's first inauguration: p. 1-2.
Second inauguration: p. 287-294.

1325

The transfer of power. Time, v. 82, Nov. 29, 1963: 25-26. illus. AP2.T37, v. 82

1326

Wise, Dan, *and* Marietta (Morris) Maxfield. The day Kennedy died. San Antonio, Naylor Co. [1964] 137 p. E842.9.W5

Swearing in of President Johnson: p. 127-130.

Lyndon B. Johnson
Second Inauguration

1327

The covenant. The inauguration. Time, v. 85, Jan. 29, 1965: 9-19A. illus. (part col.) AP2.T37, v. 85

1328

Eastern to sponsor inauguration on NBC. Sponsor, v. 18, Aug. 24, 1964: 19. HF6146.R3S6, v. 18

1329

Eller, J. N. It was a warm day in Washington. America, v. 112, Feb. 6, 1965: 185. BX801.A5, v. 112

1330

Floats prepared for inauguration. New York times, Jan. 17, 1965: 58.
Newsp

1331

For LBJ—a Texas-size inaugural. Newsweek, v. 65, Jan. 25, 1965: 21-22. illus. AP2.N6772, v. 65

1332

For the inauguration: mufti for President, quilts for newsmen. Editor & publisher, v. 97, Dec. 26, 1964: 11. PN4700.E4, v. 97

1333

Friedman, Rick. Weather, security inauguration worries. Editor & publisher, v. 98, Jan. 16, 1965: 60. illus. PN4700.E4, v. 98

1334

Gilley, Fred T. Wood to launch a President. American forests, v. 71, Jan. 1965: 2-3, 48-49. illus. SD1.A55, v. 71

1335

Great day. New Yorker, v. 40, Jan. 30, 1965: 24-25.
AP2.N6763, v. 40

1336

Great society bows in; inauguration of Lyndon B. Johnson sets tone of integration for Nation. Ebony, v. 20, Apr. 1965: 66-68, 70, 72-73. illus. (part col.) AP2.E165, v. 20

1337

Heady, Robert. Inauguration to be showcase for new marketing face of Eastern Air Lines. Advertising age, v. 36, Jan. 18, 1965: 3, 94.
HF5801.A276, v. 36

1338

Inaugural parade—how it's being changed. U.S. news & world report, v. 58, Jan. 4, 1965: 10. JK1.U65, v. 58

1339

Inaugural protection for the President: glass and armor plate. U.S. news & world report, v. 58, Jan. 11, 1965: 10. illus. JK1.U65, v. 58

1340

Inaugural–"y'all come." Newsweek, v. 65, Jan. 18, 1965: 22-23. illus.
AP2.N6772, v. 65

1341

The inauguration of President Johnson. Life, v. 58, Jan. 29, 1965: 24-33. col. illus. AP2.L547, v. 58

Color photograph of inauguration scene appears on cover of this issue.

1342

Inauguration of the President of the United States and Vice President. Congressional record, 89th Congress, 1st session, v. 111, Jan. 20, 1965: 984-986. J11.R5, v. 111

1343

Inauguration week. Time, v. 85, Jan. 22, 1965: 13. illus.
AP2.T37, v. 85

1344

Johnson dresses down; his decision to wear business suit at inauguration bucks time-honored tradition. Business week, Dec. 19, 1964: 30. illus.
HF5001.B89, 1964

1345

Johnson's inauguration broadcasters' field day. Broadcasting, v. 68, Jan. 25, 1965: 72-73. illus. TK6540.B85, v. 68

1346

Johnson's lavish inauguration. Illustrated London news, v. 246, Jan. 30, 1965: 32-35. illus. AP4.I3, v. 246

1347

Lyndon Johnson's pledge: 'I will lead, and I will do the best I can.' Hail to the Chief. Newsweek, v. 65, Feb. 1, 1965: 10-17. illus. (part col.)
AP2.N6772, v. 65

1348

Phelps, McAndrew. Portrait of the President as a reasonable man. America, v. 112, Jan. 30, 1965: 157. BX801.A5, v. 112

1349
Photo report: it was LBJ's great day. U.S. news & world report, v. 58, Feb. 1, 1965: 37-40. illus. JK1.U65, v. 58

1350
Security so tight Indians had to take heads off arrows. Washington post, Jan. 21, 1965: A2. Newsp

1351
Text of four prayers offered at ceremony. Washington post, Jan. 21, 1965: A9. Newsp

1352
Tremendous oath [by] T. R. B. New republic, v. 152, Jan. 23, 1965: 4. AP2.N624, v. 152

1353
Truntich, Paul J. Telephone men and women again meet the inaugural communications challenge. Transmitter, v. 53, Jan./Feb. 1965: 18-21. illus. TK1.T7, v. 53

1354
U.S. *President, 1963-1969 (Lyndon B. Johnson)* Inaugural address of Lyndon Baines Johnson, President of the United States, delivered at the Capitol, Washington, D.C., January 20, 1965. Washington, U.S. Govt. Print. Off., 1965. 3 p. ([U.S.] 89th Congress, 1st session. Senate document, no. 9) DLC

1355
Washington, D.C. Inaugural Committee, *1965.* The Inaugural Committee presents the program for the inauguration of Lyndon Baines Johnson, 36th President of the United States, and Hubert Horatio Humphrey, 38th Vice President of the United States, January 20, 1965. [Washington, 1965] 1 v. (unpaged) illus. (part col.) F200.W32

1356
Washington, D.C. Inaugural Committee, *1965.* Threshold of tomorrow: the Great Society; the inauguration of Lyndon Baines Johnson, 36th President of the United States, and Hubert Horatio Humphrey, 38th

Vice President of the United States, January 20, 1965. [Don R. Petit, editor-in-chief. Washington, Program and Book Committee of the 1965 Presidential Inaugural Committee, 1965] 107 p. illus. (part col.)
F200.W33 1965

Supplement ([12] p.) inserted at end.

Partial contents. The inaugural balls, by Perle Mesta (p. [48]-49). The inaugural belongs to the people, by John W. McCormack (p. 63, 104-106). The inaugural–an act of government, by Paul Aiken (p. [64]-65, 107-[108]).

1357

World's biggest TV studio; broadcasters ready to give record-breaking coverage to inauguration of President Johnson. Broadcasting, v. 68, Jan. 18, 1965: 78-79. illus. TK6540.B85, v. 52

SUPPLEMENT FOR 1969

Items in this supplement are not included in the index.

GENERAL

1a

Baker, Russell. Observer: inaugurations are rededications. New York times, Jan. 20, 1969: 20. Newsp

2a

Campion, Donald R. Of many things . . . [the inauguration of a President] America, v. 120, Jan. 18, 1969: [i]. BX801.A5, v. 120

3a

Fleming, Thomas J. Great moments in Presidential inaugurations. Reader's digest, v. 94, Jan. 1969: 64-69. col. illus. AP2.R255, v. 94

4a

An inaugural in tune with the times. U.S. news & world report, v. 66, Jan. 20, 1969: 6-7. illus. JK1.U65, v. 66

Includes remarks on earlier inaugurations.

5a

Laurent, Lawrence. Newsman's inaugural memories. Washington post, Jan. 18, 1969: B-12. illus. Newsp

Reminiscences of Bob Trout, CBS radio and TV reporter, who began covering inaugurations in 1933.

6a

Lawrence, David. Oath defines President's duties. Evening star (Washington), Jan. 20, 1969: A-11. Newsp

7a

Lee, Elinor. Inaugural ideas. Washington post, Jan. 16, 1969: D-1, D-5. Newsp

About food served at past inaugural events.

8a
Presidential inaugurals dotted with historic firsts. Christian Science monitor, Jan. 21, 1969: 3. Newsp

9a
Robertson, Nan. Inaugural momentos shown. New York times, Jan. 9, 1969: 33. Newsp

About the special exhibition on Presidential inaugurations at the Smithsonian's Museum of History and Technology.

10a
Schaden, Herman. If inaugural's passing you by, have a ball at exhibit. Evening star (Washington), Jan. 9, 1969: B-1. illus. Newsp

About the exhibition at the Smithsonian.

11a
Secrest, Meryle. Inaugural souvenirs: Smithsonian preparing a major exhibit. Washington post, Dec. 12, 1968: C-4. illus. Newsp

12a
Shenton, James. Topics: inaugurals, inspiring and otherwise. New York times, Jan. 18, 1969: 30. Newsp

13a
Three inaugural exhibits are open. Evening star (Washington) weekender, Jan. 11, 1969: 3. Newsp

14a
Welsh, James. Free-for-all fun: early inaugurals swung. Sunday star (Washington), Jan. 19, 1969: A-1, A-12. illus. Newsp

INAUGURAL ADDRESSES

15a
Inaugural addresses. *In* U.S. *Library of Congress.* Information bulletin, v. 27, Dec. 26, 1968: 759. Z733.U57I6, v. 27

About a special exhibit at the Library featuring manuscripts of the first inaugural addresses of Washington, Jefferson, Lincoln, and Theodore Roosevelt.

16a

Owsley, Clifford D. Address poses opportunity, challenge. Evening star (Washington), Jan. 20, 1969: AA-16. illus. Newsp

Accompanied by a shorter article, also relating to inaugural addresses, entitled "Invocation Tradition Began With Washington."

17a

Strout, Richard L. Inaugurals: an art form redeemed by Lincoln. Christian Science monitor, Jan. 20, 1969: 9. illus. Newsp

INAUGURAL BALLS

18a

. . . and dancing through the night. Washington post, Jan. 21, 1969: D-1, D-3. illus. Newsp

19a

Baskin, Claudia. Everyone wants to attend ball. Evening star (Washington), Dec. 20, 1968: C-3. illus. Newsp

20a

Beale, Betty. Nixon buoys 8,000. Evening star (Washington), Jan. 21, 1969: B-5. Newsp

21a

Billington, Joy. He didn't dance all night. Evening star (Washington), Jan. 21, 1969: B-2. illus. Newsp

22a

Billington, Joy. Only Washington, Johnson danced at inaugural balls. Evening star (Washington), Jan. 20, 1969: AA-18. illus. Newsp

23a

Billington, Joy. What a place for an inaugural ball. Evening star (Washington), Nov. 8, 1968: D-1, D-3. illus. Newsp

24a

Chart your own course at inaugural ball. Evening star (Washington), Jan. 9, 1969: B-8. Newsp

Table lists master of ceremonies, bands, Cabinet members and other personages who will be present, and States to be represented at each of the six locations.

25a

Cheshire, Maxine. Spectacular. Washington post, Jan. 21, 1969: D3. Newsp

Notes on the inaugural balls.

26a

Christmas, Anne. 'Forward together–' jampacked, in fact. Evening star (Washington), Jan. 21, 1969: B-1, B-4. illus. Newsp

27a

Christmas, Anne. Scampering after Nixons a night to remember. Sunday star (Washington), Jan. 26, 1969: E-2. Newsp

28a

Dance sites grow to six. Evening star (Washington), Dec. 11, 1968: F-13. Newsp

29a

Dixon, Ymelda. Good vibrations are smothered. Evening star (Washington), Jan. 21, 1969: B-6. Newsp

30a

'Formal'? Senate's 'baby.' Washington post, Jan. 19, 1969: F16. port. Newsp

About men's dress for the inaugural balls.

31a

'Honorable' covers a multitude of titles; inaugural ball committee solves problem of Agnew's two jobs. Washington post, Dec. 19, 1968: B-1, B-8. Newsp

32a

Inaugural ball invitation. Washington post, Dec. 18, 1968: D3. illus. Newsp

33a

Inaugural dress for Pat. Evening star (Washington), Jan. 8, 1969: D-2.
Newsp

34a

Inaugural spotlight. Evening star (Washington), Jan. 9, 1969: B-6. illus.
Newsp

Shows designer Earl Hargrove with sketch of Presidential box to be built at each of the six ball locations.

35a

Kernan, Michael. Women may wear pants to the balls. Washington post, Jan. 10, 1969: B2.
Newsp

Brief remarks on acceptable clothing for men and women attending inaugural balls.

36a

Lewis, Alfred E. Top police retirees to eye ball guests. Washington post, Jan. 18, 1969: E-2. port.
Newsp

This will be the 16th inaugural for Howard V. Covell, retired from the Metropolitan Police Department, who is in charge of security at the balls.

37a

Robb, Inez. In the beginning, there was one inaugural ball; and now there are—count them—six! Washington daily news, Jan. 20, 1969: 30.
Newsp

38a

Secrest, Meryle. 54,000 get invitations to six balls. Washington post, Dec. 12, 1968: C50.
Newsp

39a

Smith, Marie. The gowns. Washington post, Jan. 19, 1969: F13. illus.
Newsp

Full-length portraits of Mrs. Nixon and Mrs. Agnew in the gowns they will wear to inaugural balls.

40a

Smith, Marie. Mark Evans, Mrs. Arends are inaugural ball chairmen. Washington post, Nov. 26, 1968: B-1. ports. Newsp

41a

White tie preferred, black tie optional. Evening star (Washington), Dec. 7, 1968: A-11. Newsp

About dress for men at the 1969 inaugural balls, five of which are scheduled.

BIBLES

42a

Cronk, Sue. Cathedral to show inauguration Bibles. Washington post, Nov. 16, 1968: D23. illus. Newsp

43a

Fiske, Edward B. An official prayer service to open Nixon inauguration. New York times, Jan. 15, 1969: 49, 94. illus. Newsp

Picture shows one of the two Bibles to be used; article includes information on the use of Bibles in Presidential inaugurations.

44a

Inaugural Bibles and prayers. Evening star (Washington), Jan. 11, 1969: A-6. illus. Newsp

45a

Kilpatrick, Carroll. 'No war' Bible verse picked for Nixon oath. Washington post, Jan. 19, 1969: A-1, A-5. Newsp

46a

Washington, D.C. Cathedral of St. Peter and St. Paul. *Rare Book Library*. Presidential inaugural Bibles; catalogue of an exhibition, November 17, 1968, through February 23, 1969. [Washington] Washington Cathedral [1969] 49 p. plates. Z7770.W3

325-882 O-69—14

MUSIC

47a

Army Band practices 'spit and polish' for Inauguration Day. Washington post, Jan. 9, 1969: B-1. illus. Newsp

48a

Braaten, David. The 'zing' finally got to Nixon. Evening star (Washington), Jan. 20, 1969: C-1. illus. Newsp

About the inaugural concert.

49a

Dean, Ruth. Originally English–bandsman traces 'Hail to the Chief.' Evening star (Washington), Jan. 20, 1969: AA-14. facsim., port. Newsp

50a

Hume, Paul. Inaugural concerts. Washington post, Jan. 19, 1969: K2. illus., ports. Newsp

Describes features of some past concerts.

51a

Sears, Lawrence. Music: bells peal, the orchestra plays for inauguration. Sunday star (Washington), Jan. 19, 1969: D-4. ports. Newsp

52a

Welsh, James. All-American music set for Nixon concert. Evening star (Washington), Jan. 6, 1969: A-4. Newsp

WEATHER

53a

Inaugural weather: ships of state find launching seas stormy. Evening star (Washington), Jan. 20, 1969: A-3. Newsp

Briefly reviews inaugurations marred by bad weather.

54a

Stanford, Neal. Weather or not: rain, snow, or cold, inauguration goes on. Christian Science monitor, Dec. 17, 1968: 5. illus. Newsp

55a

Weather odds good on inauguration day. Washington post, Dec. 15, 1968: D7. Newsp

INAUGURATION OF RICHARD M. NIXON

56a

Auerbach, Stuart. Doctor volunteers to serve at fetes. Washington post, Jan. 18, 1969: E-2. Newsp

About medical aid plans for the various inaugural festivities.

57a

Beale, Betty, *and* Ymelda Dixon. Crowning moment: Mrs. Nixon is radiant. Evening star (Washington), Jan. 20, 1969: C-1, C-6. illus. Newsp

58a

Beale, Betty. Ideas for inaugural festivities are passed on to GOP. Evening star (Washington), Nov. 13, 1968: C-1. Newsp

59a

Beale, Betty. Inaugural heads teetotalers. Sunday star (Washington), Dec. 1, 1968: J-1. Newsp

60a

Bernstein, Carl. Police stress drive on streetwalkers; vice crackdown mapped for inaugural. Washington post, Jan. 10, 1969: C-1. Newsp

61a

Bernstein, Carl. Starlings get inaugural bird. Washington post, Nov. 12, 1968: C3. port. Newsp

About the inventor of a chemical compound offensive to starlings and his plans for birdproofing the route of the inaugural motorcade.

62a

Blumenthal, Fred. Nixon's inaugural—the most closely guarded: the new President and the Secret Service. Parade, Jan. 19, 1969: 10, 23-24. illus. AP2.P263, 1969

63a

Braaten, David. So you're not invited: inaugural, schmaugural! Evening star (Washington), Jan. 17, 1969: D-1, D-4. illus. Newsp

64a

Business backs the inaugural. Business week, Dec. 21, 1968: 26-28. illus., port. HF5001.B89, 1968

65a

Chapman, William. Insurance refused for inauguration. Washington post, Dec. 30, 1968: A5. Newsp

Includes some information on costs of inaugural events in recent years.

66a

Cheshire, Maxine. President-elect considers 'austere' inaugural. Washington post, Nov. 13, 1968: D1. Newsp

67a

A civil religion. Newsweek, v. 73, Feb. 3, 1969: 82. ports. AP2.N6772, v. 73

About the role of religion in the inauguration ceremony.

68a

Clashes erupt after [counterinaugural] march. Washington post, Jan. 20, 1969: A-1, A-6. illus. Newsp

69a

Costliest in history: inauguration is put at $2.5 million. Evening star (Washington), Jan. 20, 1969: AA-13. Newsp

70a

Crawford, Kenneth. Washington: quiet, please. Newsweek, v. 73, Feb. 3, 1969: 35. AP2.N6772, v. 73

71a

Cronk, Sue. No austere inauguration; Nixon reportedly makes decision for 'gala.' Washington post, Nov. 16, 1968: C-1. Newsp

72a
The day before the day before . . . Washington post, Jan. 19, 1969: F1-F2. illus. Newsp

Reports on the gala, the distinguished ladies' reception, Young America's Inaugural Salute, and the activities of antiwar demonstrators.

73a
Dean, Ruth. Gala official admits goof; seating snafu leaves an estimated 400 standing. Evening star (Washington), Jan. 20, 1969: C-2. Newsp

74a
Delaney, William. 'Not over 2 1/2 hours': inaugural parade shortened. Evening star (Washington), Nov. 15, 1968: A-1, A-4. port. Newsp

75a
Dimond, Thomas. Inaugural splurge here may climb as high as $20 million. Sunday star (Washington), Jan. 19, 1969: G-5. Newsp

An estimate of what visitors might spend.

76a
Dixon, Ymelda. Capitol a swirl of activity after swearing-in rites. Evening star (Washington), Jan. 21, 1969: B-6. illus. Newsp

77a
Dixon, Ymelda. An inaugural grows and grows. Evening star (Washington), Nov. 14, 1968: C-1. Newsp

78a
Excitement rising in D.C. for Nixon's day; weather uncertain. Sunday star (Washington), Jan. 19, 1969: A-1, A-12. Newsp

79a
Fialka, John. Inaugural security is the tightest ever. Sunday star (Washington), Jan. 19, 1969: B-1. Newsp

80a
First tide of visitors arriving for inaugural. Evening star (Washington), Jan. 17, 1969: A-1, A-6. Newsp

81a

Flor, Lee. Memo to private planes: don't come to National. Sunday star (Washington), Jan. 19, 1969: B-1. Newsp

About commercial transportation arrangements (including road and rail) for the inauguration.

82a

Fortune in furs populates parade stand. Evening star (Washington), Jan. 21, 1969: B-2. illus. Newsp

83a

Hailey, Jean R. Capital crowded for big day. Washington post, Jan. 20, 1969: A-1, A-6. Newsp

84a

Harrison, Bernie. TV's inaugural story cool and professional. Evening star (Washington), Jan. 21, 1969: D-8. Newsp

85a

Honsa, Carol. Americana will take to the streets. Washington post, Jan. 11, 1969: E-1, E-2. Newsp

About parade.

86a

Hunter, Marjorie. Inaugural invitation list is 5 miles long; computer and large staff rush plans for ceremonies. New York times, Dec. 17, 1968: 36. port. Newsp

A calendar of inaugural events and a short article on inaugural weather appear on the same page.

87a

Inaugural gowns. Washington post, Jan. 17, 1969: B-1, B-2. Newsp

On the same page is a sketch of Mrs. Nixon and the two girls showing the outfits they will wear at the inauguration and while watching the parade.

88a

Inaugural reviewing stand. Evening star (Washington), Nov. 18, 1968: B-1. illus. Newsp

Architect's sketch with caption.

89a

Inaugural setting. Washington post, Jan. 15, 1969: A-10. illus. Newsp

Picture shows east front of Capitol with inauguration platform, photographers' stand, and public seating.

90a

Inauguration. New Yorker, v. 44, Feb. 1, 1969: 27-28.
AP2.N6763, v. 44

91a

The inauguration: never again? Time, v. 93, Jan. 31, 1969: 12-13. illus.
AP2.T37, v. 93

92a

Inauguration drive. Washington post, Nov. 25, 1968: B5. port. Newsp

About efforts to raise money to finance the inauguration.

93a

Inauguration troop units total 10,000. Sunday star (Washington), Jan. 12, 1969: B-2. Newsp

94a

[Invitation to] the ceremonies attending the inauguration of the President and Vice President of the United States, January twentieth, nineteen hundred sixty-nine. [n.p., 1969?] folder. Mss

Text on p. [1]. Two portraits laid in.

95a

Johnson, Haynes. Nixon begins his Presidency in a solemn display of unity; 37th President to seek to end 'crisis of spirit.' Evening star (Washington), Jan. 20, 1969: A-1, A-6. illus. Newsp

96a

Kalb, Barry. Anti-war last hurrah? Protest leaders hope for peaceful 2 days. Sunday star (Washington), Jan. 19, 1969: B-1. Newsp

Describes planned activities of the demonstrators.

97a

Kalb, Barry, *and* Woody West. 8 protesters arrested close to parade route. Evening star (Washington), Jan. 20, 1969: A-1, A-6. illus. Newsp

98a

Kalb, Barry. Inaugural war protest to be nondisruptive. Evening star (Washington), Dec. 18, 1968: B-9. Newsp

99a

Kalb, Barry. U.S. weighing permits for inaugural protests. Sunday star (Washington), Jan. 12, 1969: B-2. Newsp

100a

Kernan, Michael. No intimacy in inaugural. Washington post, Jan. 21, 1969: D-1, D-4. illus. Newsp

101a

Kilpatrick, Carroll. Nixon day is spent on inaugural. Washington post, Jan. 9, 1969: A5. Newsp

102a

Kilpatrick, Carroll. Nixon will take oath today as 37th President; gray skies forecast for inaugural. Washington post, Jan. 20, 1969: A-1, A-6. illus., port. Newsp

103a

Kilpatrick, Carroll, *and* Don Oberdorfer. Richard M. Nixon becomes President with 'sacred commitment' to peace. Washington post, Jan. 21, 1969: A-1, A-8. illus. Newsp

Section B of this issue consists of eight pages of pictures taken during the inaugural ceremonies and parade.

104a

Kober, Barbara. Inaugural medal to be crewel work reproduction. Evening star (Washington), Dec. 7, 1968: A-11. Newsp

105a

Koprowski, Claude. Mariott [sic] hotels boost rates 10% for inaugural weekend visitors. Washington post, Jan. 9, 1969: E-1. Newsp

106a

Langbein, Fred. Telephone team makes inaugural history. Transmitter, v. 57, Jan./Feb. 1969: [i]-5. illus. TK1.T7, v. 57

107a

Lansing, Diane T. Three-day whirl to surround inaugural. Christian Science monitor, Dec. 17, 1968: 5. Newsp

108a

Let us . . . go forward together. Newsweek, v. 73, Jan. 27, 1969: 17-20. illus. AP2.N6772, v. 73

109a

Levey, Robert F. 50,000 visitors jam District for inaugural. Washington post, Jan. 19, 1969: A-1, A-4. illus. Newsp

110a

Levey, Robert F. Overtime raises cost of inaugural stands. Washington post, Dec. 9, 1968: B-1, B-8. Newsp

111a

Local unit formed for inaugural. Washington post, Dec. 31, 1968: D4. Newsp

Announces organization of a panel to promote participation of local residents in the Nixon inaugural.

112a

McCardle, Dorothy. 'Forward together' to inaugural weekend. Washington post, Jan. 12, 1969: G3. Newsp

113a

McCardle, Dorothy. From inaugural vendor to gala producer. Washington post, Jan. 4, 1969: E-1. port. Newsp

About Ed McMahon, producer of the Nixon-Agnew inaugural gala, who while a college student in 1949 operated a food vending stand on the day of Truman's inauguration.

114a

McCardle, Dorothy. New GOP is not tagging LBJ, but inaugural auto plates go to Truman, Eisenhower. Washington post, Jan. 5, 1969: E17-E18. illus. Newsp

115a

McGrory, Mary. Nixon's big moment is a muted affair. Evening star (Washington), Jan. 21, 1969: A-1, A-6. illus. Newsp

Illustrations on p. A-4, A-5.

116a

Martin, Judith. Inaugural: tickets still available to parade and gala. Washington post, Jan. 18, 1969: B-1, B-3. Newsp

117a

National Geographic Society, *Washington, D.C.* Inaugural medals–once not for sale–now prized by collectors. Washington [1968] 3 l. (National geographic news bulletin)

118a

Nixon appoints Marriott as chairman of Inaugural Committee. Evening star (Washington), Nov. 14, 1968: A-13. Newsp

119a

Nixon car pelted, 82 arrested in parade incidents. Evening star (Washington), Jan. 21, 1969: A-4. illus. Newsp

120a

Nixon garb. Washington post, Jan. 18, 1969: B3. Newsp

Clothing to be worn by Mr. and Mrs. Nixon for inaugural events.

121a

Nixon gets no. 1. Sunday star (Washington), Dec. 1, 1968: A-1. illus. Newsp

Picture shows inaugural license plate issued to the President-elect.

122a
Oakes, William. The swirl of inaugural pageantry. Christian Science monitor, Jan. 25, 1969: 9. illus. Newsp

Sketches.

123a
Plans mushroom for inauguration. Christian Science monitor, Dec. 19, 1968: 13. Newsp

Compares current plans with simplicity of arrangements for Jefferson's inaugurations.

124a
Police rolls swelled for inaugural. Washington post, Jan. 15, 1969: A-10. Newsp

125a
Police will bolster all street patrols. Washington post, Jan. 18, 1969: E-2. Newsp

126a
Radcliffe, Donnie. Maybe it's fun after all; there were moments of comedy and glory. Evening star (Washington), Jan. 21, 1969: B-1. illus. Newsp

127a
Rhetoric meets reality. Life, v. 66, Jan. 31, 1969: 18-31. col. illus. AP2.L547, v. 66

128a
Robertson, Nan. 'Astonishing room' houses inaugural group. New York times, Jan. 13, 1969: 14. illus. Newsp

About the Pension Building.

129a
Robertson, Nan. Inaugural stand takes lot of wood and work. New York times, Dec. 21, 1968: 39. illus. Newsp

130a
Ruvinsky, Aaron. Inaugural lumber slated for homes in Tennessee. Evening star (Washington), Jan. 17, 1969: C-1, C-11. illus. Newsp

131a

Schaden, Herman. Thousands line avenue to cheer under gray skies. Evening star (Washington), Jan. 20, 1969: A-7. illus. Newsp

Other pictures on p. B-1.

132a

Selover, William S. Hippies 'salute' Inauguration Day. Christian Science monitor, Jan. 22, 1969: 3. illus. Newsp

133a

Shelton, Isabelle. Gala scene goes mad: some tickets had no seat. Sunday star (Washington), Jan. 19, 1969: E-5. illus. Newsp

134a

Sherwood, John. The Rambler: . . . and Jan. 20, 1969. Evening star (Washington), Jan. 21, 1969: D-1. Newsp

135a

Sidelights: establishment fuels 'counter inaugural.' Evening star (Washington), Jan. 20, 1969: A-8. Newsp

Includes brief reports on several other incidents relating to the inauguration.

136a

Smith, Marie. Inauguration Day, 1969: the hails . . . Washington post, Jan. 21, 1969: D-1, D-2. illus. Newsp

137a

Smith, Marie. Three days of festivities to celebrate Nixon inauguration. Washington post, Dec. 4, 1968: B-1. ports. Newsp

138a

Somervelle, Gerald. 25 cents to $45: Nixon souvenirs run gamut. Evening star (Washington), Jan. 17, 1969: D-1. illus. Newsp

139a

Spencer, Duncan. Nixon stands going to Johnson City; Charlie Smith: matchmaker for men, material. Evening star (Washington), Feb. 13, 1969: B-1, B-6. illus. Newsp

About the disposition of the lumber from the inaugural stands.

140a

Strout, Richard L. A plea for unity: 'I shall consecrate my office, my energies, and wisdom to the cause of world peace.' Christian Science monitor, Jan. 21, 1969: 1, 11. illus. Newsp

141a

Swanston, Walterene. Early parade arrivals came prepared for wait. Evening star (Washington), Jan. 20, 1969: A-3. Newsp

142a

Toward the Nixon inauguration. Time, v. 93, Jan. 17, 1969: 13-14. illus. AP2.T37, v. 93

143a

250,000 applaud parade; protesters clash with police. Washington post, Jan. 21, 1969: A-1, A-10. illus. Newsp

144a

U.S. *Congress. Joint Committee on Arrangements for the Inauguration, 1969.* Inauguration ceremonies program, January twentieth, nineteen hundred sixty-nine. [n.p., 1969?] [9] p. Mss

Accompanied by ticket to "admit bearer to the Inaugural Stands, East Front of Capitol."

145a

U.S. *President, 1969- (Nixon)* Inaugural address of Richard Milhous Nixon, President of the United States, delivered at the Capitol, Washington, D.C., January 20, 1969. Washington, U.S. Govt. Print. Off., 1969. 5 p. ([U.S.] 91st Congress, 1st session. Senate document no. 91-3)

146a

Valentine, Paul W. Agreement near on parade plan of counter-inaugural. Washington post, Jan. 16, 1959: E3. Newsp

147a

Valentine, Paul W. Peace group maps 'inaugural march.' Washington post, Dec. 19, 1968: D-1. Newsp

148a

Valentine, Paul W. Post-Chicago confrontation: inaugural faces 1st major protest. Washington post, Jan. 18, 1969: A-1, A-13. illus.
Newsp

149a

Wanderings. Washington post, Jan. 10, 1969: B4. illus. Newsp

Describes the grandstands being built in the 1600 block of Pennsylvania Avenue, N.W., in preparation for the inaugural parade.

150a

Washington, D.C. Inaugural Committee, *1969.* Forward together; official guide book, inaugural 1969. [Washington, 1969?] 32 p. illus., map, ports.

151a

Washington: white-tie inaugural. Newsweek, v. 72, Dec. 23, 1968: 22. illus.
AP2.N6772, v. 72

152a

Weil, Martin. Counter-inaugural opens in bubbling bedlam. Washington post, Jan. 19, 1969: A4. illus.
Newsp

153a

Weil, Martin. Inaugural marchers hail phantom notables. Washington post, Jan. 13, 1969: B-1. illus.
Newsp

Another illustration on p. A-1.

154a

Welsh, James. Nixon masters the art of parade reviewing. Evening star (Washington), Jan. 21, 1969: D-1, D-2. illus.
Newsp

155a

Welsh, James. Surplus from inaugural may reach $500,000. Evening star (Washington), Jan. 16, 1969: C-2.
Newsp

156a

When Nixon takes over ... U.S. news & world report, v. 66, Jan. 6, 1969: 7. illus.
JK1.U65, v. 66

157a
Whittemore, Reed. Washington interregnum. Washington post, Jan. 21, 1969: D-2. port. Newsp

Poem.

158a
With lowered voice, enter Mr. Nixon. Newsweek, v. 73, Feb. 3, 1969: 16-21. col. illus. AP2.N6772, v. 73

159a
Wright, Chris. Pickpockets beware: police getting inaugural aid. Evening star (Washington), Jan. 14, 1969: B-12. Newsp

160a
Wright, Chris. Some Capital visitors coming to play games–badger variety, that is. Evening star (Washington), Jan. 17, 1969: A-9. Newsp

INDEX

Supplementary items 1a-160a are not represented in the index.

A

325-882 O-69—15

C

F

G

T

U

V

W

U.S. GOVERNMENT PRINTING OFFICE : 1969 O—325-882